C000196290

Carnivore Diet Cookbook for Beginners

The Complete Guide to Carnivore Diet: 300 Yummy Carnivore

Recipes to Reset & Energize Your Body

Stiven Pown

Table of Contents

Introduction

This is book is one of the right choices for you if you love to eat meats, steak, ribs, and more. I think many of you are aware of the carnivore diet and its benefits. This book will guide you to adopt a carnivore diet properly. The carnivore diet depends on animal-based products. The diet allows you to consume meats comes from any source. Plant-based foods are strictly avoided in this diet. If you follow the ketogenic diet then you have noticed many similarities between the carnivore and keto diet. Both the diet is a low cab diet and allows them to consume high-fat foods.

The carnivore diet is simple to follow as compared to the keto diet it is a less restrictive diet plan. While following a carnivore diet you never need to count macros, calories, meal timing, and so on. The carnivore diet is basically a zero-carb diet and very effective for weight loss purposes. The diet comes with various health benefits like it improves your brainpower, treats epilepsy condition, controls your blood sugar, improves your heart health, and more. The book contains the basics of a carnivore diet and a list of foods that are allowed and avoid during diet along with the health benefits of the diet.

The book contains healthy and delicious recipes comes from different categories like breakfast, poultry, beef, pork & lamb, fish & seafood, snack, and salad. All the carnivore diet recipes written in this book are unique and written in an easily understandable form. The recipes written in this book are in standard format with their serving size, exact preparation, and cooking time followed by cooking instructions. All the recipes end with their nutritional value information. The nutritional value information helps you to track your daily calorie consumption. There are lots of cookbooks available in the market on this diet thanks for choosing my book. I hope you have love and enjoy all the recipes written in this book and the book helps you to achieve your goal by successfully adopting the carnivore diet.

Chapter 1: The Basics of Carnivore Diet

What is Carnivore Diet?

The name carnivore itself tells us about the diet. The carnivore diet is a high-fat high protein diet completely based on only the consumption of animal food and their by-products. That means you cannot eat vegetarian products like vegetables, fruits, nuts, grains, legumes, etc. Instead of this, the carnivore diet allows only to eat meat, beef, eggs, fish, and their by-products such as butter, cheese, dairy products. It also allows eating zero calories food such as spices and coffee. The carnivore diet is the same as a near keto diet plan which restricts the carb consumption during the diet.

The carnivore diet is also known as zero carb diet plans which only allow you to eat meat eggs or dairy products during the diet period. The diet allows you to consume as many fats and proteins you gain from the daily meal except carbohydrates. Basically, the carnivore diet is a high protein and low carb diet plan. Many research and study prove that reducing the crabs from the diet has many health benefits such as weight loss, improve your digestion, control blood sugar level, decrease the risk of cardiovascular disease, increase your energy level and stamina. The low carb diet is not only improves your physical health but also helps to improve your mental health.

What to Eat During a Carnivore Diet?

The carnivore diet basically starts from only eating meats and completely avoids vegetables and other carb foods.

Here is the list of the recommended food during a carnivore diet:

- Meat: There are lots of choices available in the meat you can use grass-fed meats, beef, red meats, fatty cuts, steak, pork chops, bacon, porterhouse, and more. In the absence of carbohydrates, your body completely depends on the nutrients that come from meat intake. During the carnivore diet, high-fat meat cuts are recommended because our body depends on fats for energy. Grass-fed meat is recommended during carnivore diet and avoids processed meat and meat products.

- Fish: During the carnivore diet almost all types of fish are allowed during diet. It is recommended that high-fat fish are one of the best options available. You can eat fish like salmon, halibut, haddock, sardines, mackerel, trout, and catfish.
- Organ Meats: Most of the carnivore diet follower considers organ meat is beneficial for the development of your brain. They prefer to eat cold-water fish, brain, liver, and fish oil like codfish. All these are enriched with DHA fatty acids which help to improve your brain functioning.
- Eggs: Eggs are nutritious and it provides a balanced source of fats, proteins, and essential nutrients to our body. So during carnivore diet eggs are important and act as nature's multivitamin.
- Dairy: The dairy products are coming from animals and allowed to use during the carnivore diet. You can consume milk, full-fat cheese, yogurt, and grass-fed butter. Most of the carnivore followers minimize dairy consumption due to lactose content most of the people avoided due to food intolerance. Dairy food is important during the diet because they add lots of nutrients to your diet.
- Bone Marrow: Bone broth is one of the best sources of protein and rich in minerals which helps to improve your joint health. It also includes vitamins and fatty acids.
- Condiments: The carnivore diet only recommended using salt, pepper, & spices taken with a piece of fatty meats and bone broth.
- Beverages: The diet allows you to consume bone broth, water, coffee, and tea in this category. If your goal is to lose weight then you can take coffee and some tea during the diet. Take these kinds of beverages in limit because excess intake of caffeine dehydrates your body during the diet. During the carnivore diet, it is recommended to drink 2.4 liters of water daily for getting long term health benefits. Most of the diet followers only prefer to drink water in the first 30 days. Add little sea salt to add some extra electrolyte into the water.

How Much Food Eats During a Carnivore Diet?

There are no restrictions on eating food during the carnivore diet. You can eat as much food as you can feel full. It is recommended to eat at least two full meals per day. Try to add fatty meal into your diet, as per carnivore diet guideline you must consume 2 pounds of fatty meat per day. If you perform daily heavy work then you should consume 4 pounds of fatty meals per day during the diet period. Do not restrict your daily food consumption during a carnivore diet; eat as many fatty meals as you want.

Foods Avoid During Carnivore Diet

Here is the list of foods that do not comes from animal sources and high in carb values are avoided during the carnivore diet. These foods are:

- **Vegetables:** Carrots, spinach, potatoes, peppers, broccoli, cauliflower, green beans, etc.
- **Fruits:** Apple, kiwi, oranges, bananas, berries, avocado, etc.
- **Nuts & seeds:** Pumpkin seeds, almonds, pistachios, sunflower seeds, sesame seeds, walnuts, pecans, etc.
- **Grains:** Wheat, rice, bread, cereals, pasta, quinoa, etc.
- **Legumes:** Peanuts, lentils, beans, etc.
- **Sugar:** Maple syrup, agave syrup, brown sugar, table sugar, etc.
- **Plant-based oils:** Coconut oil, sunflower oil, canola oil, olive oil, etc.
- **Alcohol:** Liquor, beer, wine, etc.

Benefits of Carnivore Diet

If you follow the carnivore diet in a proper way then you have experienced various health benefits that come from the diet. All these benefits are given as follows:

1. **Weight loss**

As we know the keto diet is one of the meat base diets that help to reduce excess bodyweight rapidly. Due to the carb restriction and high fat intake, your body shifts itself to breakdown fats for energy. When your metabolism adapted fat then your body pushes into ketosis. Your metabolism allows using both dietary and stored fats for fuel. This indicates that your body is now ready to burn its own fat for energy. In this fat burning process, you have noticed that your body weight decreases rapidly during the carnivore diet.

2. **Increase Testosterone**

One of the scientific research study conducted by American Journal of Clinical Nutrition found that the peoples who followed the diet which is high in fat and low in fiber for 10 weeks found 13 % increase in testosterone as compared to the peoples who eat low protein high fiber food. The high-fat diet helps to increase the testosterone level in many cases. Carnivore diet allows you to consume healthy fats and proteins during the diet. The healthy fat gain will regulate your testosterone hormone level.

3. Improves brain functions

When your body breaks down fats for energy ketones are used as a primary source of energy. These ketones are one of the best fuels for your brain. It full fills more than 70 percent of your daily brain energy needs. Carnivore diet not only improves your physical health but also improves your brain functions. According to the study if you increase intake of your meat protein and decrease the intake of carb from your diet will help to improve your reaction time.

4. Effective of certain medical conditions

The high-fat low carb diet is very effectively curing certain medical conditions like epilepsy, diabetes, autism, cancer, and heart-related disease. The carnivore diet is rich in omega 3 fatty acid, cysteine (protein building block), vitamin D&B which helps to improve the endometriosis condition.

5. Reduce Inflammation

The study and research show that the low carb diet is more effective than the low-fat diet. It reduces the level of saturated fatty acids in your blood and helps to reduce the markers of inflammation. The high carb foods cause to increase the inflammatory response in your body. The carnivore diet is a less inflammatory diet which leads to less pain.

6. Improves cardiovascular health

Grass-fed meat or red meat is one of the healthy options in the carnivore diet. Processed meat and food are responsible for the heart-related disease. When you consume too much-processed foods it increases the LDL level in your body. LDL is also known as bad cholesterol which increases the risk of heart-related disease. On the other side when you are on a carnivore diet it helps to increase the HDL (good cholesterol) level in your body and decrease the LDL level which helps to improve your heart condition and cardiovascular health.

FAQs

1. **What food allowed during the carnivore diet?**

Only animal meats including fats muscles and organs meat which are high in fat. Grass-fed and red meat is the best options available to start a carnivore diet.

2. **How much eat during the diet?**

There is no restriction on eating meat during the diet. You can eat as much as meat until you feel full. It is recommended that eat 2 to 4 pounds of meat per day during a carnivore diet.

3. **How many fats and proteins should eat per day?**

When you are on a carnivore diet you should eat around 70 to 80 % of fats and 20 to 30 % of protein consumption per day. You have consumed a total of 2000 calories in one day

4. **How much time taken to see the diet results?**

It takes a few days to a few weeks after the successful adaptation of diet. You will notice the changes like improving the energy level, sleep, digestion, skin, and more. Health benefits of the carnivore diet.

5. **Should I take supplements during the diet?**

The supplement needs it depends on your daily nutritional needs. If you talk about whey protein then it is not required during the diet because there is plenty of proteins are found in meat and beef. You can take supplements like vitamins and minerals to improve your health.

6. **Can I eat Processed Meat during Diet?**

No, always prefer to eat grass-fed animal products instead of processed products. The processed meat contains artificial nitrates to preserve the food which is harmful to your health.

Chapter 2: Breakfast

Breakfast Waffle

Preparation Time: 10 minutes
Cooking Time: 6 minutes
Serve: 1

Ingredients:

- 1 egg
- ½ cup ground pork rinds
- 1/3 cup mozzarella cheese, shredded
- Pinch of salt

Directions:

1. Preheat the waffle iron.
2. In a bowl, whisk egg, pork rinds, shredded cheese, and salt.
3. Pour waffle mixture into the center of the waffle iron and cook for 3-5 minutes.
4. Serve and enjoy.

Nutritional Value (Amount per Serving):

- Calories 90
- Fat 6 g
- Carbohydrates 0.7 g
- Sugar 0.3 g
- Protein 8.2 g
- Cholesterol 169 mg

Bacon Cheese Quiche

Preparation Time: 10 minutes
Cooking Time: 22 minutes
Serve: 8

Ingredients:

- 6 eggs
- 1 ½ cups Colby jack cheese, grated
- 6 bacon slices, cooked & crumbled
- 2/3 cup heavy cream
- Pepper
- Salt

Directions:

1. Preheat the oven to 350 F.
2. In a bowl, whisk eggs with 1 cup Colby jack cheese, bacon, heavy cream, pepper, and salt.
3. Pour egg mixture into the baking dish and bake in preheated oven for 19 minutes.
4. Sprinkle remaining cheese on top and bake for 1-2 minutes more.
5. Serve and enjoy.

Nutritional Value (Amount per Serving):

- Calories 216
- Fat 19 g
- Carbohydrates 2 g
- Sugar 1 g
- Protein 11 g
- Cholesterol 175 mg

Ham Cheese Quiche

Preparation Time: 10 minutes
Cooking Time: 40 minutes
Serve: 6

Ingredients:

- 8 eggs
- 1/2 cup heavy cream
- 1 cup cheddar cheese, shredded
- 1 cup ham, cooked and diced
- Pepper
- Salt

Directions:

1. Preheat the oven to 375 F.
2. Combine ham and cheddar cheese in a baking dish.
3. In a bowl, whisk eggs, heavy cream, pepper, and salt.
4. Pour egg mixture over ham mixture.
5. Bake for 40 minutes.
6. Serve and enjoy.

Nutritional Value (Amount per Serving):

- Calories 231
- Fat 17.7 g
- Carbohydrates 1.8 g
- Sugar 0.3 g
- Protein 0.6 g
- Cholesterol 265 mg

Perfect Breakfast Chaffle

Preparation Time: 10 minutes
Cooking Time: 6 minutes
Serve: 2

Ingredients:

- 1 egg, lightly beaten
- 1/2 cup mozzarella cheese, shredded

Directions:

1. In a bowl, whisk eggs with cheese.
2. Brush waffle iron with butter.
3. Pour half egg mixture into the hot waffle iron and cook for 2-3 minutes.
4. Remove chaffle and cook the remaining batter.
5. Serve and enjoy.

Nutritional Value (Amount per Serving):

- Calories 51
- Fat 3.4 g
- Carbohydrates 0.4 g
- Sugar 0 g
- Protein 0.2 g
- Cholesterol 86 mg

Cheese Bacon Chaffle

Preparation Time: 10 minutes
Cooking Time: 12 minutes
Serve: 4

Ingredients:

- 2 eggs, lightly beaten
- 2 bacon slices, cooked and chopped
- 3/4 cup cheddar cheese, shredded

Directions:

1. Heat waffle maker and brush with melted butter.
2. In a bowl, whisk eggs with bacon, and cheese.
3. Pour 1/4 of the batter into the hot waffle maker and cook for 3 minutes.
4. Serve and enjoy.

Nutritional Value (Amount per Serving):

- Calories 168
- Fat 13.2 g
- Carbohydrates 0.6 g
- Sugar 0 g
- Protein 0.3 g
- Cholesterol 115 mg

Cheddar Chicken Chaffle

Preparation Time: 10 minutes
Cooking Time: 8 minutes
Serve: 2

Ingredients:

- 1 egg
- 1/3 cup cheddar cheese, shredded
- 1/3 cup chicken, cooked and chopped
- Pepper
- Salt

Directions:

1. A heat waffle iron.
2. In a medium bowl, whisk the egg with pepper and salt.
3. Add chicken and shredded cheese and mix until well combined.
4. Add half of the mixture into the hot waffle iron and cook for 4 minutes or until cooked through.
5. Serve and enjoy.

Nutritional Value (Amount per Serving):

- Calories 143
- Fat 9.1 g
- Carbohydrates 0.4 g
- Sugar 0.3 g
- Protein 14.2 g
- Cholesterol 120 mg

Tuna Chaffle

Preparation Time: 10 minutes
Cooking Time: 8 minutes
Serve: 2

Ingredients:

- 1 egg
- 2.5 oz can tuna, drained
- 1/2 cup mozzarella cheese, shredded
- Pepper
- Salt

Directions:

1. Heat waffle maker.
2. In a small bowl, whisk the egg with pepper and salt.
3. Add cheese and tuna and mix well.
4. Pour 1/2 of the mixture into the hot waffle maker and cook for 4 minutes.
5. Serve and enjoy.

Nutritional Value (Amount per Serving):

- Calories 93
- Fat 3.7 g
- Carbohydrates 0.5 g
- Sugar 0.2 g
- Protein 13.8 g
- Cholesterol 96 mg

Mexican Chicken Cheese Chaffle

Preparation Time: 10 minutes
Cooking Time: 8 minutes
Serve: 2

Ingredients:

- 1 egg
- 1/2 cup Mexican cheese, shredded
- 4 oz chicken breast, cooked and chopped
- 1 tbsp mayonnaise

Directions:

1. Heat waffle iron and lightly grease with butter.
2. In a mixing bowl, mix together egg, cheese, mayonnaise, and chicken.
3. Pour 1/2 of the batter into the hot waffle maker and cook for 4 minutes or until cooked.
4. Serve and enjoy.

Nutritional Value (Amount per Serving):

- Calories 205
- Fat 13.3 g
- Carbohydrates 2.7 g
- Sugar 0.6 g
- Protein 19.7 g
- Cholesterol 140 mg

Breakfast Egg Cups

Preparation Time: 10 minutes
Cooking Time: 25 minutes
Serve: 12

Ingredients:

- 12 eggs
- 12 bacon strips, uncooked
- 2/3 cup cheddar cheese, shredded
- 4 oz cream cheese
- Pepper
- Salt

Directions:

1. In a bowl, whisk eggs, pepper, and salt.
2. Line each muffin cup with one bacon strip.
3. Pour egg mixture into each muffin cup and bake at 375 F for 10 minutes.
4. In another bowl, mix cheddar cheese and cream cheese and microwave for 30 seconds.
5. Remove muffin tray from the oven and add 2 tsp cheese mixture in the center of each egg cup.
6. Return muffin tray to the oven and cook for 15 minutes more.
7. Serve and enjoy.

Nutritional Value (Amount per Serving):

- Calories 221
- Fat 18.8 g
- Carbohydrates 0.7 g
- Sugar 0.4 g
- Protein 11.8 g
- Cholesterol 181 mg

Sausage Egg Muffins

Preparation Time: 10 minutes
Cooking Time: 25 minutes
Serve: 12

Ingredients:

- 6 eggs
- 1/2 cup mozzarella cheese
- 1 cup cheddar cheese
- 1 cup egg whites
- 1 lb ground pork sausage
- Pepper
- Salt

Directions:

1. Preheat the oven to 350 F.
2. Brown sausage over medium-high heat.
3. Divide cheese and cooked sausages into each muffin cups.
4. In a large bowl, whisk together egg whites, egg, pepper, and salt.
5. Pour egg mixture into each muffin cups.
6. Bake for 25 minutes.
7. Serve and enjoy.

Nutritional Value (Amount per Serving):

- Calories 203
- Fat 15.6 g
- Carbohydrates 0.5 g
- Sugar 0.4 g
- Protein 14.3 g
- Cholesterol 126 mg

Breakfast Egg Bake

Preparation Time: 10 minutes
Cooking Time: 25 minutes
Serve: 8

Ingredients:

- 6 eggs, lightly beaten
- 1 cup cheddar cheese, shredded
- 1 lb sausage
- 1/2 tsp black pepper
- 1/2 tsp salt

Directions:

1. Preheat the oven to 375 F.
2. Brown sausage in a pan over medium heat.
3. In a bowl, whisk eggs, cheese, pepper, and salt.
4. Add sausage to the baking dish and pour the egg mixture on top.
5. Bake for 25 minutes or until lightly golden brown.
6. Serve and enjoy.

Nutritional Value (Amount per Serving):

- Calories 168
- Fat 13.2 g
- Carbohydrates 0.6 g
- Sugar 0 g
- Protein 0.3 g
- Cholesterol 115 mg

Egg Scrambled

Preparation Time: 10 minutes
Cooking Time: 10 minutes
Serve: 4

Ingredients:

- 6 eggs
- 2 tbsp butter
- 3 oz cheddar cheese, shredded
- Pepper
- Salt

Directions:

1. Melt butter in a pan over medium heat.
2. Whisk eggs in a bowl and pour into the pan and scramble for 2 minutes.
3. Add cheese and stir well.
4. Season with pepper and salt.
5. Serve and enjoy.

Nutritional Value (Amount per Serving):

- Calories 231
- Fat 19.4 g
- Carbohydrates 0.8 g
- Sugar 0.6 g
- Protein 13.7 g
- Cholesterol 283 mg

Chapter 3: Poultry

Delicious Chicken Soup

Preparation Time: 10 minutes
Cooking Time: 10 minutes
Serve: 3

Ingredients:

- 2 chicken breasts, skinless and boneless
- 2 tbsp butter
- 1/2 tsp garlic powder
- 3 cups chicken broth
- 1 cup heavy cream
- 2 cups cheddar cheese, shredded
- Pepper
- Salt

Directions:

1. Add all ingredients except cheese and heavy cream into the instant pot and stir well.
2. Secure pot with lid and cook on high for 10 minutes.
3. Once done, release pressure using quick-release then remove the lid.
4. Remove chicken from pot and shred the chicken using a fork.
5. Return shredded chicken into the pot and stir well.
6. Add cheese and cream and stir to combine.
7. Serve and enjoy.

Nutritional Value (Amount per Serving):

- Calories 734
- Fat 56 g
- Carbohydrates 3.4 g
- Sugar 1.3 g
- Protein 52.8 g
- Cholesterol 241 mg

Cheesy Bacon Chicken

Preparation Time: 10 minutes
Cooking Time: 12 minutes
Serve: 8

Ingredients:

- 2 lbs chicken breasts, skinless and boneless
- 1 cup chicken broth
- 1/4 cup bacon, chopped
- 4 oz cream cheese, cubed

Directions:

1. Set the instant pot on sauté mode.
2. Add bacon into the pot and sauté for 3-4 minutes.
3. Add remaining ingredients into the instant pot and stir well.
4. Secure pot with lid and cook on high for 12 minutes.
5. Once done, release pressure using quick-release then remove the lid.
6. Shred the chicken using a fork and stir well.
7. Serve and enjoy.

Nutritional Value (Amount per Serving):

- Calories 270
- Fat 13.8 g
- Carbohydrates 0.5 g
- Sugar 0.1 g
- Protein 34.7 g
- Cholesterol 117 mg

Garlic Chicken

Preparation Time: 10 minutes
Cooking Time: 12 minutes
Serve: 8

Ingredients:

- 2 lbs chicken breasts, skinless and boneless
- 1 cup chicken broth
- 1 tbsp garlic, chopped
- 1/2 tsp salt

Directions:

1. Add all ingredients into the instant pot and mix well.
2. Secure pot with lid and cook on high for 12 minutes.
3. Once done, allow to release pressure naturally then remove the lid.
4. Remove chicken from pot.
5. Using a fork shred the chicken.
6. Return shredded chicken into the pot and stir well.
7. Serve and enjoy.

Nutritional Value (Amount per Serving):

- Calories 222
- Fat 8.6 g
- Carbohydrates 0.5 g
- Sugar 0.1 g
- Protein 33.5 g
- Cholesterol 101 mg

Herb Chicken Breasts

Preparation Time: 10 minutes
Cooking Time: 13 minutes
Serve: 4

Ingredients:

- 2 lbs chicken breasts, skinless and boneless
- 1 tbsp Dijon mustard
- 1 tsp sage, dried
- 1 tbsp rosemary, dried
- 1 tsp thyme, dried
- 1 cup buttermilk
- 1/2 tsp pepper
- 1/2 tsp salt

Directions:

1. In a bowl, add all ingredients and mix until chicken is well coated.
2. Place marinated chicken in the refrigerator for 1 hour.
3. Pour marinated chicken into the instant pot.
4. Secure pot with lid and cook on high for 13 minutes.
5. Once done, release pressure using quick-release then remove the lid.
6. Serve and enjoy.

Nutritional Value (Amount per Serving):

- Calories 463
- Fat 17.7 g
- Carbohydrates 4.1 g
- Sugar 3 g
- Protein 67.9 g
- Cholesterol 204 mg

Bacon Herb Chicken

Preparation Time: 10 minutes
Cooking Time: 8 hours
Serve: 4

Ingredients:

- 5 chicken breasts
- 5 tbsp butter, melted
- 2 tbsp thyme, dried
- 10 bacon slices
- 1 tbsp rosemary, dried
- 1 tbsp oregano, dried
- 1 tbsp salt

Directions:

1. Add all ingredients into the slow cooker and mix well.
2. Cover and cook on low for 8 hours.
3. Shred the chicken using a fork and serves.

Nutritional Value (Amount per Serving):

- Calories 741
- Fat 48.1 g
- Carbohydrates 2.8 g
- Sugar 0.1 g
- Protein 70.8 g
- Cholesterol 253 mg

Chicken Casserole

Preparation Time: 10 minutes
Cooking Time: 40 minutes
Serve: 8

Ingredients:

- 2 lbs cooked chicken, shredded
- 6 oz cream cheese, softened
- 4 oz butter, melted
- 6 oz ham, cut into small pieces
- 5 oz Swiss cheese
- 1 tbsp Dijon mustard
- 1/2 tsp salt

Directions:

1. Preheat the oven to 350 F.
2. Arrange chicken in the baking dish then layer ham pieces on top.
3. Add butter, mustard, cream cheese, and salt into the blender and blend until a thick sauce.
4. Spread sauce over top of chicken and ham mixture in the baking dish.
5. Arrange Swiss cheese slices on top of sauce.
6. Bake for 40 minutes.
7. Serve and enjoy.

Nutritional Value (Amount per Serving):

- Calories 450
- Fat 29.2 g
- Carbohydrates 2.4 g
- Sugar 0.3 g
- Protein 43 g
- Cholesterol 170 mg

Baked Chicken Wings

Preparation Time: 10 minutes
Cooking Time: 60 minutes
Serve: 4

Ingredients:

- 2 lbs chicken wings
- 1/4 tsp garlic powder
- 1/8 tsp paprika
- 2 tsp seasoned salt

Directions:

1. Preheat the oven to 400 F.
2. In a mixing bowl, add all ingredients except chicken wings and mix well.
3. Add chicken wings to the bowl mixture and coat well and place on a baking tray.
4. Bake 60 minutes or until cooked through.
5. Serve and enjoy.

Nutritional Value (Amount per Serving):

- Calories 432
- Fat 16.8 g
- Carbohydrates 0.2 g
- Sugar 0.1 g
- Protein 65.7 g
- Cholesterol 202 mg

Tasty Greek Chicken

Preparation Time: 10 minutes
Cooking Time: 20 minutes
Serve: 4

Ingredients:

- 4 chicken breasts, skinless and boneless
- 1 tsp dried rosemary
- 1 tbsp dried oregano
- 1 tbsp ginger garlic paste
- 1/4 cup butter, melted
- 1/2 tsp paprika
- 1 tsp dried parsley
- 1 tsp dried thyme
- 1/4 tsp pepper
- 1 tsp salt

Directions:

1. Add all ingredients except chicken to the large bowl and mix well.
2. Add chicken to the bowl and coat well and place it in the refrigerator for 1 hour.
3. Remove chicken from the refrigerator.
4. Place marinated chicken on hot grill and cook for 6-7 minutes on each side.
5. Slice and serve.

Nutritional Value (Amount per Serving):

- Calories 392
- Fat 22.8 g
- Carbohydrates 2.1 g
- Sugar 0.1 g
- Protein 42.8 g
- Cholesterol 160 mg

Tasty Chicken Skewers

Preparation Time: 10 minutes
Cooking Time: 20 minutes
Serve: 4

Ingredients:

- 1 1/2 lbs chicken breast, cut into 1-inch cubes

For marinade:

- 2 tbsp dried oregano
- 5 garlic cloves
- 1/4 tsp cayenne
- 1 cup butter, melted
- 1 tbsp red wine vinegar
- 1/2 cup yogurt
- 2 tbsp fresh rosemary, chopped
- Pepper
- Salt

Directions:

1. Add all marinade ingredients into the blender and blend until smooth.
2. Pour marinade into a large bowl.
3. Add chicken to the bowl and coat well and place it in the refrigerator for 1 hour.
4. Preheat the oven to 400 F.
5. Remove marinated chicken from the refrigerator and slide onto the skewers.
6. Place skewers on grill and cooks for 15-20 minutes.
7. Serve and enjoy.

Nutritional Value (Amount per Serving):

- Calories 642
- Fat 51.2 g
- Carbohydrates 6.1 g
- Sugar 2.4 g
- Protein 38.9 g
- Cholesterol 233 mg

Easy Turkey Patties

Preparation Time: 10 minutes
Cooking Time: 10 minutes
Serve: 2

Ingredients:

- 8 oz ground turkey
- 1 garlic clove, chopped
- 1 egg, lightly beaten
- Pepper
- Salt

Directions:

1. Add all ingredients into the mixing bowl and mix until well combined.
2. Make two large patties from the mixture.
3. Spray pan with cooking spray and heat over medium heat.
4. Place patties on the hot pan and cook for 4-5 minutes on each side.
5. Serve and enjoy.

Nutritional Value (Amount per Serving):

- Calories 255
- Fat 14.7 g
- Carbohydrates 0.7 g
- Sugar 0.2 g
- Protein 33.9 g
- Cholesterol 198 mg

Parmesan Chicken

Preparation Time: 10 minutes
Cooking Time: 25 minutes
Serve: 4

Ingredients:

- 4 chicken breasts, skinless and boneless
- 1/4 cup parmesan cheese, grated
- 1/4 cup mayonnaise, fat-reduced

Directions:

1. Preheat the oven to 375 F.
2. Spread mayo on both sides of the chicken breast.
3. Coat chicken with cheese and place in baking dish.
4. Bake for 20-25 minutes.
5. Serve and enjoy.

Nutritional Value (Amount per Serving):

- Calories 353
- Fat 16.9 g
- Carbohydrates 3.7 g
- Sugar 0.9 g
- Protein 44.2 g
- Cholesterol 138 mg

Cheese Garlic Chicken

Preparation Time: 10 minutes
Cooking Time: 25 minutes
Serve: 2

Ingredients:

- 2 chicken breasts, skinless and boneless
- 1/4 cup parmesan cheese, shredded
- 1/2 cup mozzarella cheese, shredded
- 1 tsp dried parsley
- 2 garlic cloves, minced
- 1/4 cup butter
- Pepper
- Salt

Directions:

1. Preheat the oven to 400 F.
2. Season chicken with pepper and salt and place in a baking dish.
3. Melt butter in a pan over low heat.
4. Add garlic and sauté for 30 seconds.
5. Remove pan from heat and let it cool.
6. Pour butter mixture over chicken. Sprinkle with dried parsley.
7. Bake for 20 minutes.
8. Sprinkle mozzarella cheese and parmesan cheese on top of chicken mixture and bake for 5 minutes more.
9. Serve and enjoy.

Nutritional Value (Amount per Serving):

- Calories 506
- Fat 37.5 g
- Carbohydrates 1.7 g
- Sugar 0.1 g
- Protein 48.3 g
- Cholesterol 203 mg

Moist & Juicy Chicken Breasts

Preparation Time: 10 minutes
Cooking Time: 10 minutes
Serve: 2

Ingredients:

- 2 chicken breasts, boneless
- 1/8 tsp cayenne
- 1/4 tsp paprika
- 1/4 tsp dried parsley
- 1/4 tsp garlic powder
- 1 tbsp butter, melted
- Salt

Directions:

1. Preheat the air fryer to 380 F.
2. Brush chicken breasts with melted butter.
3. In a small bowl, mix garlic powder, parsley, paprika, cayenne pepper, and salt and rub all over chicken breasts.
4. Place chicken breasts in the air fryer basket and cook for 10 minutes. Turn chicken halfway through.
5. Serve and enjoy.

Nutritional Value (Amount per Serving):

- Calories 331
- Fat 16.6 g
- Carbohydrates 0.5 g
- Sugar 0.1 g
- Protein 42.4 g
- Cholesterol 145 mg

Flavorful Chicken Wings

Preparation Time: 10 minutes
Cooking Time: 25 minutes
Serve: 4

Ingredients:

- 1 lb chicken wings
- 1 tsp garlic powder
- 1/4 tsp pepper
- 1/2 tsp salt
- For sauce:
- 1/8 tsp garlic powder
- 1 tbsp butter, melted

Directions:

1. Preheat the air fryer to 390 F.
2. In a mixing bowl, toss chicken wings with garlic powder, pepper, and salt.
3. Add chicken wings into the air fryer basket and cook for 25 minutes.
4. In a large bowl, mix together melted butter and garlic powder.
5. Add chicken wings and toss until well coated.
6. Serve and enjoy.

Nutritional Value (Amount per Serving):

- Calories 244
- Fat 11.3 g
- Carbohydrates 0.7 g
- Sugar 0.2 g
- Protein 33 g
- Cholesterol 109 mg

Tasty Chicken Nuggets

Preparation Time: 10 minutes
Cooking Time: 25 minutes
Serve: 4

Ingredients:

- 1 1/2 lbs chicken breast, boneless & cut into chunks
- 1/4 cup parmesan cheese, shredded
- 1/4 cup mayonnaise
- 1/2 tsp garlic powder
- 1/4 tsp salt

Directions:

1. Preheat the air fryer to 400 F.
2. In a mixing bowl, mix mayonnaise, cheese, garlic powder, and salt.
3. Add chicken and mix until well coated.
4. Add chicken to the air fryer basket and cook for 25 minutes.
5. Serve and enjoy.

Nutritional Value (Amount per Serving):

- Calories 270
- Fat 10.4 g
- Carbohydrates 4 g
- Sugar 1 g
- Protein 38.1 g
- Cholesterol 117 mg

Garlic Pepper Chicken

Preparation Time: 10 minutes
Cooking Time: 30 minutes
Serve: 4

Ingredients:

- 4 chicken breasts, skinless and boneless
- 1 tsp granulated garlic
- 1 tbsp ground pepper
- 1 tsp salt

Directions:

1. Preheat the air fryer to 360 F.
2. Sprinkle chicken with pepper, granulated garlic, and salt.
3. Add chicken to the air fryer basket and cook for 30 minutes. Turn chicken halfway through.
4. Serve and enjoy.

Nutritional Value (Amount per Serving):

- Calories 284
- Fat 10.9 g
- Carbohydrates 1.6 g
- Sugar 0.2 g
- Protein 42.5 g
- Cholesterol 130 mg

Simple Chicken Drumsticks

Preparation Time: 10 minutes
Cooking Time: 25 minutes
Serve: 6

Ingredients:

- 6 chicken drumsticks
- 1/2 tsp dried parsley
- 1/2 tsp garlic powder
- 2 tbsp butter, melted
- Pepper
- Salt

Directions:

1. Preheat the air fryer to 400 F.
2. Add chicken drumsticks and butter in a large bowl and toss well.
3. Sprinkle garlic powder, parsley, and salt over chicken drumsticks and toss until well coated.
4. Arrange chicken drumsticks in the air fryer basket and cook for 25 minutes.
5. Serve and enjoy.

Nutritional Value (Amount per Serving):

- Calories 113
- Fat 6.5 g
- Carbohydrates 0.2 g
- Sugar 0.1 g
- Protein 12.7 g
- Cholesterol 51 mg

Stuffed Chicken

Preparation Time: 10 minutes
Cooking Time: 30 minutes
Serve: 4

Ingredients:

- 4 chicken breasts, boneless & cut a pocket into the side of chicken breast
- 2 tbsp butter, melted
- 1 tsp dried parsley
- 2 oz mozzarella cheese, shredded
- 2 oz feta cheese, crumbled
- 4 oz cream cheese
- Pepper
- Salt

Directions:

1. Preheat the oven to 400 F.
2. In a small bowl, mix cream cheese, parsley, mozzarella cheese, and feta cheese until well combined.
3. Stuff cream cheese mixture into each chicken breast and secure edges with toothpicks.
4. Season chicken with pepper and salt and brush with butter.
5. Place stuff chicken breasts on a baking tray and bake 30 minutes.
6. Serve and enjoy.

Nutritional Value (Amount per Serving):

- Calories 505
- Fat 32 g
- Carbohydrates 1.9 g
- Sugar 0.6 g
- Protein 50.5 g
- Cholesterol 197 mg

Parmesan Garlic Chicken Wings

Preparation Time: 10 minutes
Cooking Time: 2 hours 30 minutes
Serve: 8

Ingredients:

- 2 lbs chicken wings
- 1 tbsp garlic, minced
- 1/2 stick butter, melted
- 1 1/2 cups parmesan cheese, grated
- 1 1/2 tsp dried parsley
- Pepper
- Salt

Directions:

1. Add chicken wings into the slow cooker.
2. Mix 1 cup grated cheese, parsley, garlic, butter, pepper, and salt and pour over chicken wings.
3. Cover and cook on high for 2 hours 30 minutes.
4. Transfer chicken wings on a baking tray.
5. Sprinkle with remaining cheese and broil for 5 minutes.
6. Serve and enjoy.

Nutritional Value (Amount per Serving):

- Calories 322
- Fat 17.8 g
- Carbohydrates 1 g
- Sugar 0 g
- Protein 38.4 g
- Cholesterol 128 mg

Easy Grilled Chicken Patties

Preparation Time: 10 minutes
Cooking Time: 10 minutes
Serve: 4

Ingredients:

- 1 lb ground chicken
- 1/2 tsp garlic powder
- 1/2 tsp dried parsley
- Pepper
- Salt

Directions:

1. Preheat the grill.
2. Add all ingredients into the large bowl and mix well to combine.
3. Make patties from mixture and place on hot grill and cook for 5 minutes on each side.
4. Serve and enjoy.

Nutritional Value (Amount per Serving):

- Calories 220
- Fat 8 g
- Carbohydrates 1 g
- Sugar 0.5 g
- Protein 32 g
- Cholesterol 100 mg

Garlic Rosemary Chicken

Preparation Time: 10 minutes
Cooking Time: 35 minutes
Serve: 4

Ingredients:

- 4 chicken breasts, skinless
- 1 tsp rosemary, chopped
- 1/2 tsp garlic, chopped
- 1/4 cup chicken broth
- 1/2 tbsp butter, melted
- Pepper
- Salt

Directions:

1. Preheat the oven to 450 F.
2. Rub chicken with garlic and butter. Season with rosemary and pepper.
3. Place chicken in the baking dish.
4. Pour broth around the chicken and bake for 25 minutes.
5. Flip chicken and bake for 10 minutes more.
6. Serve and enjoy.

Nutritional Value (Amount per Serving):

- Calories 230
- Fat 9 g
- Carbohydrates 2 g
- Sugar 1 g
- Protein 33 g
- Cholesterol 100 mg

Parmesan Chicken Breasts

Preparation Time: 10 minutes
Cooking Time: 35 minutes
Serve: 4

Ingredients:

- 1 lb chicken breasts, skinless and boneless
- 1 cup mayonnaise
- 1 tsp garlic powder
- 1 tsp dried parsley
- 1/2 cup parmesan cheese, grated
- Pepper
- Salt

Directions:

1. Preheat the oven to 375 F.
2. In a small bowl, mix mayonnaise, garlic powder, dried parsley, pepper, and salt.
3. Place chicken into the baking dish.
4. Pour mayo mixture over chicken and sprinkle grated cheese on top.
5. Bake for 35 minutes.
6. Serve and enjoy.

Nutritional Value (Amount per Serving):

- Calories 390
- Fat 22 g
- Carbohydrates 10 g
- Sugar 3 g
- Protein 30 g
- Cholesterol 110 mg

Feta Cheese Chicken Breasts

Preparation Time: 10 minutes
Cooking Time: 45 minutes
Serve: 8

Ingredients:

- 8 chicken breasts, skinless and boneless
- 1 tbsp oregano
- 3 oz feta cheese, crumbled
- Pepper
- Salt

Directions:

1. Preheat the oven to 350 F.
2. Place chicken in a baking dish.
3. Mix together remaining ingredients and pour over chicken and bake for 45 minutes.
4. Serve and enjoy.

Nutritional Value (Amount per Serving):

- Calories 244
- Fat 10 g
- Carbohydrates 1 g
- Sugar 1 g
- Protein 35 g
- Cholesterol 110 mg

Herb Chicken Breast

Preparation Time: 10 minutes
Cooking Time: 12 minutes
Serve: 4

Ingredients:

- 1 lb chicken breasts, skinless and boneless
- 1 tbsp garlic, chopped
- 2 tsp dried mix herbs
- 3 cups chicken broth
- Pepper
- Salt

Directions:

1. Season chicken with dried mix herbs, pepper, and salt and place in the instant pot.
2. Add remaining ingredients over chicken.
3. Secure pot with lid and cook on high for 12 minutes.
4. Once done, release pressure using the quick-release method. Remove lid.
5. Serve and enjoy.

Nutritional Value (Amount per Serving):

- Calories 150
- Fat 4 g
- Carbohydrates 1 g
- Sugar 0.5 g
- Protein 25 g
- Cholesterol 68 mg

Cheesy Chicken Breasts

Preparation Time: 10 minutes
Cooking Time: 4 hours
Serve: 4

Ingredients:

- 1 lb chicken breasts, skinless and boneless
- 2 tbsp butter, melted
- 1/2 cup chicken broth
- 1/2 tsp pepper
- 1 tsp oregano, dried
- 1 tsp thyme, dried
- 1 tsp rosemary, dried
- 1/2 cup ricotta cheese
- 4 oz cream cheese
- 1 tbsp garlic, minced

Directions:

1. Place chicken into the slow cooker.
2. Top with ricotta cheese and cream cheese.
3. Pour remaining ingredients over chicken.
4. Cover and cook on high for 4 hours.
5. Serve and enjoy.

Nutritional Value (Amount per Serving):

- Calories 424
- Fat 28 g
- Carbohydrates 4 g
- Sugar 0.5 g
- Protein 39 g
- Cholesterol 140 mg

Chapter 4: Beef

Beef Tacos

Preparation Time: 10 minutes
Cooking Time: 60 minutes
Serve: 4

Ingredients:

- 1 1/2 lbs beef roast
- 1 cup beef stock
- Pepper
- Salt

Directions:

1. Place the beef roast into the instant pot.
2. Add remaining ingredients into the pot.
3. Secure pot with a lid and selects manual and cook for 60 minutes.
4. Once done release pressure using quick release then remove the lid.
5. Remove meat from pot and shred using a fork.
6. Serve and enjoy.

Nutritional Value (Amount per Serving):

- Calories 320
- Fat 10.7 g
- Carbohydrates 0 g
- Sugar 0 g
- Protein 52.3 g
- Cholesterol 152 mg

Easy Shredded Beef

Preparation Time: 10 minutes
Cooking Time: 1 hour 30 minutes
Serve: 6

Ingredients:

- 3 lbs chuck roast
- 1 tsp oregano
- 1/2 tsp ground ginger
- 2 tsp garlic powder
- 4 garlic cloves
- 1/4 cup vinegar
- 1 cup beef stock
- 1 tsp basil
- 1 tsp sea salt

Directions:

1. Using a knife make slits on chuck roast and stuff garlic in each slit.
2. In a small bowl, mix garlic powder, basil, oregano, ginger, and salt.
3. Rub garlic powder mixture over roast and place in the instant pot.
4. Pour vinegar and stock into the pot.
5. Secure pot with a lid and select manual and cook for 90 minutes.
6. Once done, allow to release pressure naturally then remove the lid.
7. Remove meat from pot and shred using a fork.
8. Serve and enjoy.

Nutritional Value (Amount per Serving):

- Calories 502
- Fat 19 g
- Carbohydrates 1.7 g
- Sugar 0.3 g
- Protein 75.7 g
- Cholesterol 229 mg

Flavors Beef Skewers

Preparation Time: 10 minutes
Cooking Time: 8 minutes
Serve: 4

Ingredients:

- 2 lbs beef sirloin, cut into cubes
- 1/4 cup butter, melted
- 2 tsp fresh thyme, minced
- 1 tbsp fresh parsley, minced
- 4 garlic cloves, minced
- 2 tsp dried oregano
- 2 tsp fresh rosemary, minced
- Pepper
- Salt

Directions:

1. Add all ingredients except meat in a bowl and stir everything well.
2. Add meat to the bowl and coat well with marinade.
3. Place in refrigerator overnight.
4. Preheat the grill medium-high heat.
5. Slide marinated meat onto the skewers and grill for 6-8 minutes. Turn after every 2 minutes.
6. Serve and enjoy.

Nutritional Value (Amount per Serving):

- Calories 534
- Fat 25.9 g
- Carbohydrates 2.3 g
- Sugar 0.1 g
- Protein 69.3 g
- Cholesterol 233 mg

Beef Tips

Preparation Time: 10 minutes
Cooking Time: 20 minutes
Serve: 4

Ingredients:

- 1 lb sirloin, cut into chunks
- 1 1/2 tbsp oregano
- 2 tbsp butter, melted
- 2 garlic cloves, crushed
- Pepper
- Salt

Directions:

1. Add meat, garlic, oregano, butter, pepper, and salt in a bowl and stir well to coat. Cover bowl and place in refrigerator overnight.
2. Grill marinated beef tips on hot grill over medium-high heat until cooked.
3. Serve and enjoy.

Nutritional Value (Amount per Serving):

- Calories 269
- Fat 13 g
- Carbohydrates 1.6 g
- Sugar 0.1 g
- Protein 34.8 g
- Cholesterol 117 mg

Tasty Chuck Roast

Preparation Time: 10 minutes
Cooking Time: 10 hours
Serve: 6

Ingredients:

- 2 lbs beef chuck roast
- 1/2 cup beef broth
- 25 garlic cloves, peeled
- 2 tbsp vinegar

Directions:

1. Place meat into the slow cooker.
2. Pour remaining ingredients over meat.
3. Cover and cook on low for 10 hours.
4. Remove meat from slow cooker and shred using a fork.
5. Return shredded meat to the slow cooker and stir well.
6. Serve and enjoy.

Nutritional Value (Amount per Serving):

- Calories 572
- Fat 42.2 g
- Carbohydrates 4.3 g
- Sugar 0.2 g
- Protein 40.8 g
- Cholesterol 156 mg

Savory Shredded Beef

Preparation Time: 10 minutes
Cooking Time: 35 minutes
Serve: 4

Ingredients:

- 1 lb beef chuck roast
- 1 cup beef broth
- 2 tbsp butter, melted
- 1 tbsp balsamic vinegar
- 1 tsp oregano
- 1 tsp thyme
- 1 tbsp garlic, minced
- Pepper
- Salt

Directions:

1. Add butter into the instant pot and set the pot on sauté mode.
2. Add garlic and sauté for a minute.
3. Add meat and sear for 2 minutes.
4. Season with thyme, oregano, pepper, and salt.
5. Add balsamic vinegar and broth and stir well.
6. Secure pot with lid and cook on high for 30 minutes.
7. Once done, allow to release pressure naturally then remove the lid.
8. Shred the meat using a fork.
9. Serve and enjoy.

Nutritional Value (Amount per Serving):

- Calories 478
- Fat 37.7 g
- Carbohydrates 1.4 g
- Sugar 0.2 g
- Protein 31.1 g
- Cholesterol 132 mg

Meatballs

Preparation Time: 10 minutes
Cooking Time: 20 minutes
Serve: 6

Ingredients:

- 2 lbs ground beef
- 1 egg, lightly beaten
- 1/2 tsp allspice
- 1 tsp oregano
- 1 tsp cinnamon
- 1 tsp garlic, minced
- 1/4 tsp pepper
- 1/2 tsp salt

Directions:

1. Preheat the oven to 400 F.
2. Add all ingredients into the large mixing bowl and mix until well combined.
3. Make small balls from the meat mixture and place onto the baking tray.
4. Bake for 15-20 minutes.
5. Serve and enjoy.

Nutritional Value (Amount per Serving):

- Calories 294
- Fat 10.2 g
- Carbohydrates 0.9 g
- Sugar 0.1 g
- Protein 46.9 g
- Cholesterol 162 mg

Beef Stew Meat

Preparation Time: 10 minutes
Cooking Time: 40 minutes
Serve: 6

Ingredients:

- 3 lbs beef stew meat
- 1 tbsp dried oregano
- 1/2 cup beef broth
- 2 tbsp vinegar
- 2 garlic cloves
- 1 tbsp butter, melted
- 1/2 tsp pepper
- 3/4 tsp salt

Directions:

1. Add butter into the instant pot and set the pot on sauté mode.
2. Add meat to the pot and sauté until browned.
3. Add remaining ingredients and stir well.
4. Secure pot with lid and cook on high for 30 minutes.
5. Once done then allow to release pressure naturally then remove the lid.
6. Shred the meat using a fork and stir well.
7. Serve and enjoy.

Nutritional Value (Amount per Serving):

- Calories 447
- Fat 16.3 g
- Carbohydrates 1.1 g
- Sugar 0.1 g
- Protein 69.4 g
- Cholesterol 208 mg

Steak Bites

Preparation Time: 10 minutes
Cooking Time: 20 minutes
Serve: 6

Ingredients:

- 2 3/4 lbs round steak, cut into bites
- 1/4 cup butter, melted
- 1/4 tsp pepper
- 2 garlic cloves, minced
- 1 cup beef stock
- 1/2 tsp salt

Directions:

1. Add all ingredients to the instant pot and stir well.
2. Secure pot with lid and cook on high for 20 minutes.
3. Once done then release pressure using the quick-release then remove the lid.
4. Stir well and serve.

Nutritional Value (Amount per Serving):

- Calories 521
- Fat 27.8 g
- Carbohydrates 0.4 g
- Sugar 0 g
- Protein 63.3 g
- Cholesterol 197 mg

Tasty Flank Steak

Preparation Time: 10 minutes
Cooking Time: 15 minutes
Serve: 4

Ingredients:

- 1 1/2 lbs flank steak, cut into strips
- 1/4 tsp oregano
- 1 1/2 tsp paprika
- 2 tbsp butter, melted
- 3 garlic cloves, minced
- 1/2 cup chicken stock
- Pepper
- Salt

Directions:

1. Season meat with pepper and salt.
2. Add butter into the instant pot and set the pot on sauté mode.
3. Add meat and sauté until brown.
4. Add remaining ingredients and stir to combine.
5. Secure pot with lid and cook on high for 15 minutes.
6. Once done then allow to release pressure naturally then remove the lid.
7. Shred the meat using a fork and serve.

Nutritional Value (Amount per Serving):

- Calories 388
- Fat 20.1 g
- Carbohydrates 1.4 g
- Sugar 0.2 g
- Protein 47.7 g
- Cholesterol 109 mg

Tender Country Style Ribs

Preparation Time: 10 minutes
Cooking Time: 35 minutes
Serve: 4

Ingredients:

- 2 lbs country-style spareribs, boneless
- 1 tbsp liquid smoke
- 14 oz can chicken stock
- 1 tbsp sea salt

Directions:

1. Season spareribs with sea salt and set aside.
2. Add liquid smoke and broth into the instant pot.
3. Place spareribs into the pot.
4. Secure pot with lid and cook on meat mode for 35 minutes.
5. Once done then release pressure using the quick-release method than remove the lid.
6. Serve and enjoy.

Nutritional Value (Amount per Serving):

- Calories 658
- Fat 55.4 g
- Carbohydrates 3.5 g
- Sugar 1.6 g
- Protein 38.6 g
- Cholesterol 184 mg

Meatballs

Preparation Time: 10 minutes
Cooking Time: 20 minutes
Serve: 6

Ingredients:

- 1 lb ground beef
- 1 egg, lightly beaten
- 1 tbsp fresh basil, chopped
- 1 tbsp fresh parsley, chopped
- 1 tbsp fresh rosemary, chopped
- 2 garlic cloves, minced
- 1/4 cup parmesan cheese, grated
- Pepper
- Salt

Directions:

1. Preheat the oven to 375 F.
2. Add all ingredients into the mixing bowl and mix until well combined.
3. Make small balls from the meat mixture and place them on a cooking tray.
4. Bake for 20 minutes.
5. Serve and enjoy.

Nutritional Value (Amount per Serving):

- Calories 155
- Fat 6.3 g
- Carbohydrates 0.9 g
- Sugar 0.1 g
- Protein 25.2 g
- Cholesterol 98 mg

Cheesy Baked Burger Patties

Preparation Time: 10 minutes
Cooking Time: 15 minutes
Serve: 6

Ingredients:

- 2 lbs ground beef
- 1 tsp garlic powder
- 1 cup mozzarella cheese, grated
- Pepper
- Salt

Directions:

1. Preheat the oven to 400 F.
2. Add all ingredients into the large bowl and mix until well combined.
3. Make patties from meat mixture and place on a cooking tray.
4. Bake for 15 minutes.
5. Serve and enjoy.

Nutritional Value (Amount per Serving):

- Calories 296
- Fat 10.3 g
- Carbohydrates 0.5 g
- Sugar 0.1 g
- Protein 47.3 g
- Cholesterol 138 mg

Meatballs

Preparation Time: 10 minutes
Cooking Time: 20 minutes
Serve: 4

Ingredients:

- 1 lb ground beef
- 1 tbsp rosemary, chopped
- 2 tbsp milk
- 1 egg, lightly beaten
- 2 garlic cloves, minced
- 1 tsp dried basil
- 1/4 cup parmesan cheese, grated
- Pepper
- Salt

Directions:

1. Preheat the oven to 375 F.
2. Add all ingredients into the bowl and mix until well combined.
3. Make small balls from the meat mixture and place them on a cooking tray.
4. Bake for 20 minutes.
5. Serve and enjoy.

Nutritional Value (Amount per Serving):

- Calories 253
- Fat 9.7 g
- Carbohydrates 1.7 g
- Sugar 0.4 g
- Protein 38 g
- Cholesterol 147 mg

Delicious Beef Tacos

Preparation Time: 10 minutes
Cooking Time: 6 hours
Serve: 8

Ingredients:

- 2 lbs round roast, cut into chunks
- 2 tbsp butter, melted
- 1 cup chicken stock
- 1 tsp garlic, minced
- 1 tsp salt

Directions:

1. Heat butter in a pan over medium heat.
2. Add meat and cook until browned from all the sides.
3. Transfer meat to the slow cooker.
4. Pour remaining ingredients over meat.
5. Cover and cook on high for 6 hours.
6. Shred the meat using a fork and serve.

Nutritional Value (Amount per Serving):

- Calories 239
- Fat 11.7 g
- Carbohydrates 0.2 g
- Sugar 0.1 g
- Protein 31.2 g
- Cholesterol 105 mg

Mustard Chuck Roast

Preparation Time: 10 minutes
Cooking Time: 6 hours
Serve: 8

Ingredients:

- 3 lbs beef chuck roast, cut into 1-inch cubes
- 1 tsp garlic powder
- 2 1/2 tbsp yellow mustard
- 4 oz heavy cream
- 1 tsp salt

Directions:

1. Add heavy cream, garlic powder, mustard, and salt into the slow cooker and stir well.
2. Add meat and stir to coat.
3. Cover and cook on low for 6 hours.
4. Serve and enjoy.

Nutritional Value (Amount per Serving):

- Calories 671
- Fat 52.8 g
- Carbohydrates 0.9 g
- Sugar 0.2 g
- Protein 45.1 g
- Cholesterol 195 mg

Beef Patties

Preparation Time: 10 minutes
Cooking Time: 10 minutes
Serve: 6

Ingredients:

- 1 lb ground beef
- 1 lb ground lamb
- 2 tbsp butter, melted
- 1 tsp dried rosemary
- 1 tbsp dried oregano
- 1 tbsp dried thyme
- 1 tsp pepper
- 1 1/2 tsp salt

Directions:

1. Add all ingredients into the large bowl and mix until well combined.
2. Make even shape patties from meat mixture.
3. Grill patties over medium heat for 5 minutes on each side.
4. Serve and enjoy.

Nutritional Value (Amount per Serving):

- Calories 326
- Fat 15.1 g
- Carbohydrates 1.1 g
- Sugar 0 g
- Protein 44.3 g
- Cholesterol 136 mg

Simple Beef Roast

Preparation Time: 10 minutes
Cooking Time: 10 hours
Serve: 6

Ingredients:

- 5 lbs beef roast
- 2 tbsp garlic, minced
- 1 stick butter
- Pepper
- Salt

Directions:

1. Place the beef roast into the slow cooker.
2. Sprinkle garlic, pepper, and salt over the roast.
3. Place butter on top of the roast.
4. Cover and cook on low for 10 hours.
5. Using a fork shred the meat.
6. Serve and enjoy.

Nutritional Value (Amount per Serving):

- Calories 841
- Fat 38.8 g
- Carbohydrates 1 g
- Sugar 0 g
- Protein 115 g
- Cholesterol 378 mg

Meatballs

Preparation Time: 10 minutes
Cooking Time: 20 minutes
Serve: 6

Ingredients:

- 2 lbs ground beef
- 1 egg, lightly beaten
- 1 tsp oregano
- 1/2 tsp dried parsley
- 1/2 tsp dried thyme
- 1 tsp cinnamon
- 1 tsp garlic, minced
- 1/4 tsp pepper
- 1/2 tsp salt

Directions:

1. Preheat the oven to 400 F.
2. Add all ingredients into the large mixing bowl and mix until well combined.
3. Make small balls from the meat mixture and place them on a baking tray.
4. Bake in for 15-20 minutes.
5. Serve and enjoy.

Nutritional Value (Amount per Serving):

- Calories 294
- Fat 10.2 g
- Carbohydrates 0.8 g
- Sugar 0.1 g
- Protein 46.9 g
- Cholesterol 162 mg

Roasted Sirloin Steak

Preparation Time: 10 minutes
Cooking Time: 40 minutes
Serve: 6

Ingredients:

- 2 lbs sirloin steak, cut into 1-inch cubes
- 2 garlic cloves, minced
- 1 tsp dried oregano
- 1/4 cup water
- 1/4 cup butter, melted
- 1/2 tsp black pepper
- 1 tsp salt

Directions:

1. Add all ingredients except beef into the large bowl and mix well.
2. Pour bowl mixture into the large zip-lock bag.
3. Add beef to the bag and shake well and place it in the refrigerator for 1 hour.
4. Preheat the oven to 400 F.
5. Place marinated beef on a baking tray and bake for 30 minutes.
6. Serve and enjoy.

Nutritional Value (Amount per Serving):

- Calories 365
- Fat 18 g
- Carbohydrates 2 g
- Sugar 0.4 g
- Protein 45 g
- Cholesterol 135 mg

Chapter 5: Pork & Lamb

Rosemary Garlic Leg of Lamb

Preparation Time: 10 minutes
Cooking Time: 35 minutes
Serve: 8

Ingredients:

- 3 lbs leg of lamb, boneless
- 2 cups of water
- 2 tbsp butter, melted
- 2 tbsp fresh rosemary, chopped
- 3 garlic cloves, crushed
- Pepper
- Salt

Directions:

1. Season lamb with pepper and salt.
2. Add butter into the instant pot and set the pot on sauté mode.
3. Add lamb to the pot and cook until browned.
4. Remove lamb from the pot.
5. Add rosemary and garlic to the pot.
6. Pour water into the pot then place the rack into the pot.
7. Place lamb on top of the rack.
8. Secure pot with lid and cook on meat/stew mode for 35 minutes.
9. Once done then allow to release pressure naturally for 10 minutes then release using the quick-release. Remove the lid.
10. Slice and serve.

Nutritional Value (Amount per Serving):

- Calories 350
- Fat 15 g
- Carbohydrates 0.9 g
- Sugar 0 g
- Protein 47.9 g
- Cholesterol 153 mg

Lamb Shanks

Preparation Time: 10 minutes
Cooking Time: 38 minutes
Serve: 6

Ingredients:

- 1 1/2 lbs lamb shanks, chopped
- 2 tbsp butter
- 1 cup chicken stock
- 2 tsp rosemary powder
- 1 tbsp garlic powder
- Pepper
- Salt

Directions:

1. Rub lamb shanks with rosemary, garlic, pepper, and salt.
2. Add butter into the instant pot and set the pot on sauté mode.
3. Add shanks to the pot and cook until browned.
4. Add stock. Secure pot with lid and cook on high for 30 minutes.
5. Once done then release pressure using the quick-release than remove the lid.
6. Secure pot on sauté mode and cook for 3 minutes until sauce thickened.
7. Serve and enjoy.

Nutritional Value (Amount per Serving):

- Calories 355
- Fat 17 g
- Carbohydrates 10.6 g
- Sugar 0.6 g
- Protein 37.2 g
- Cholesterol 112 mg

Dinner Lamb Shoulder

Preparation Time: 10 minutes
Cooking Time: 1 hour 30 minutes
Serve: 6

Ingredients:

- 4 lbs lamb shoulder, bone-in
- 1 tsp dried oregano
- 1 tsp garlic, minced
- 2 cups chicken stock
- 2 tsp butter, melted
- Salt

Directions:

1. Add butter into the instant pot and set the pot on sauté mode.
2. Add lamb into the pot and cook until browned from both sides.
3. Remove lamb from the pot and set aside.
4. Add stock and garlic to the pot and stir.
5. Return meat to the pot and season with oregano and salt.
6. Secure pot with lid and cook on high for 90 minutes.
7. Once done then allow to release pressure naturally for 10 minutes then release using the quick-release. Remove the lid.
8. Slice and serve.

Nutritional Value (Amount per Serving):

- Calories 600
- Fat 24.8 g
- Carbohydrates 0.6 g
- Sugar 0.3 g
- Protein 88.5 g
- Cholesterol 285 mg

Parmesan Lamb Chops

Preparation Time: 10 minutes
Cooking Time: 18 minutes
Serve: 3

Ingredients:

- 3 lamb chops
- 1/4 tsp dried basil, crushed
- 1 cup of water
- 1/4 tsp dried oregano, crushed
- 1/2 tsp garlic powder
- 1 tbsp butter, melted
- 3/4 cup parmesan cheese
- Pepper
- Salt

Directions:

1. Season lamb chops with pepper, garlic powder, and salt.
2. Place lamb chops into the instant pot and cook for 4 minutes on each side.
3. Remove lamb chops from pot and place on a plate.
4. Pour water into the pot then place a trivet in the pot.
5. Place lamb chops on the trivet.
6. Secure pot with lid and cook on high for 10 minutes.
7. Once done then release pressure using the quick-release then remove the lid.
8. Serve and enjoy.

Nutritional Value (Amount per Serving):

- Calories 530
- Fat 19 g
- Carbohydrates 10.5 g
- Sugar 2 g
- Protein 45 g
- Cholesterol 160 mg

Herb Pork Chops

Preparation Time: 10 minutes
Cooking Time: 30 minutes
Serve: 4

Ingredients:

- 4 pork chops, boneless
- 3 garlic cloves, minced
- 1 tsp dried rosemary, crushed
- 1/4 tsp pepper
- 1/4 tsp salt

Directions:

1. Preheat the oven to 425 F.
2. Spray a baking tray with cooking spray and set aside.
3. Season pork chops with pepper and salt and set aside.
4. In a small bowl, mix garlic and rosemary and rub over pork chops.
5. Place pork chops on baking tray and roast for 10 minutes.
6. Turn heat to 350 F and roast for 25 minutes more.
7. Serve and enjoy.

Nutritional Value (Amount per Serving):

- Calories 261
- Fat 19.9 g
- Carbohydrates 1 g
- Sugar 0 g
- Protein 18.1 g
- Cholesterol 69 mg

Spiced Pork Tenderloin

Preparation Time: 10 minutes
Cooking Time: 35 minutes
Serve: 6

Ingredients:

- 2 lbs pork tenderloin
- 2 garlic cloves, chopped
- Pepper
- Salt

For the spice mix:

- 1/2 tsp allspice
- 1 tsp cinnamon
- 1/4 tsp cayenne
- 1 tsp oregano
- 1/4 tsp cloves

Directions:

1. Preheat the oven to 375 F.
2. In a small bowl, mix together all spice ingredients and set aside.
3. Using a sharp knife make slits on pork tenderloin and inserts chopped garlic into each slit.
4. Rub spice mixture over pork tenderloin.
5. Sprinkle with pepper and salt.
6. Spray a baking tray with cooking spray.
7. Place pork tenderloin on a baking tray and bake for 30-35 minutes.
8. Slice and serve.

Nutritional Value (Amount per Serving):

- Calories 222
- Fat 5.5 g
- Carbohydrates 1.2 g
- Sugar 0.1 g
- Protein 39.8 g
- Cholesterol 110 mg

Garlic Pork Roast

Preparation Time: 10 minutes
Cooking Time: 75 minutes
Serve: 4

Ingredients:

- 2 lbs pork sirloin roast
- 2 tbsp butter, melted
- 4 garlic cloves, sliced
- 1/2 tsp pepper
- 1 tsp salt

Directions:

1. Preheat the oven to 250 F.
2. Using a sharp knife make slits on top of the roast and stuff sliced garlic in each slit.
3. Season pork roast with pepper and salt.
4. Heat butter in a pan over medium-high heat.
5. Place roast on the hot pan and cook until brown from all the sides.
6. Transfer pork roast on a baking tray and roast for 60-70 minutes. Turn roast halfway through.
7. Slice and serve.

Nutritional Value (Amount per Serving):

- Calories 526
- Fat 27.2 g
- Carbohydrates 1.2 g
- Sugar 0 g
- Protein 64.9 g
- Cholesterol 210 mg

Garlic Herb Pork Medallions

Preparation Time: 10 minutes
Cooking Time: 15 minutes
Serve: 4

Ingredients:

- 2 lbs pork tenderloin, sliced into medallions
- 1 tsp dried oregano
- 1/2 tsp dried parsley
- 3 garlic cloves, minced
- 1 1/2 tsp red wine vinegar
- 3 tbsp butter, melted
- Pepper
- Salt

Directions:

1. Add all ingredients into the large zip-lock bag, seal bag, and shake well and place it in the refrigerator for 2 hours.
2. Spray grill pan with cooking spray and heat over medium-high heat.
3. Place marinated pork medallions in the pan and cook until lightly golden brown from both sides, about 4 minutes on each side.
4. Serve and enjoy.

Nutritional Value (Amount per Serving):

- Calories 406
- Fat 16.7 g
- Carbohydrates 1 g
- Sugar 0.1 g
- Protein 59.6 g
- Cholesterol 188 mg

Baked Pork Tenderloin

Preparation Time: 10 minutes
Cooking Time: 30 minutes
Serve: 6

Ingredients:

- 2 lbs pork tenderloin

For rub:

- 1 tbsp garlic powder
- 1 tbsp smoked paprika
- 1/2 tsp salt

Directions:

1. Preheat the oven to 425 F.
2. In a small bowl, mix all rub ingredients.
3. Coat pork tenderloin with the rub.
4. Heat ovenproof pan over medium-high heat.
5. Spray pan with cooking spray.
6. Sear pork on all sides until lightly golden brown.
7. Place pan into the oven and roast for about 25-30 minutes.
8. Slice and serve.

Nutritional Value (Amount per Serving):

- Calories 224
- Fat 5.5 g
- Carbohydrates 1.7 g
- Sugar 0.5 g
- Protein 40 g
- Cholesterol 110 mg

Greek Pork Chops

Preparation Time: 10 minutes
Cooking Time: 10 minutes
Serve: 2

Ingredients:

- 2 pork chops, boneless
- 1 tsp garlic, minced
- 2 tbsp butter, melted
- 4 oz feta cheese, crumbled
- 1 tbsp dried oregano

Directions:

1. Heat butter in a pan over medium heat.
2. Add pork, oregano, and garlic to the pan and cook for 3-4 minutes.
3. Turn pork chops to another side.
4. Cover and cook for 3-4 minutes more.
5. Serve and enjoy.

Nutritional Value (Amount per Serving):

- Calories 516
- Fat 43.7 g
- Carbohydrates 4.2 g
- Sugar 2.4 g
- Protein 26.5 g
- Cholesterol 150 mg

Grilled Pork Chops

Preparation Time: 10 minutes
Cooking Time: 10 minutes
Serve: 4

Ingredients:

- 4 pork chops, bone-in
- 1/3 cup butter, melted
- 1 tsp dried thyme
- 2 tsp dried rosemary, crumbled
- 2 tsp dried sage, crumbled
- 1 1/2 tsp salt

Directions:

1. In a bowl, mix sage, thyme, rosemary, and salt.
2. Rub pork chops with herb mixture and coat with butter and place in the refrigerator overnight.
3. Preheat the grill over medium heat.
4. Lightly spray the grill with cooking spray.
5. Place marinated pork chops on hot grill and cook until lightly brown and meat is no longer pink, about 4 minutes on each side.
6. Serve and enjoy.

Nutritional Value (Amount per Serving):

- Calories 395
- Fat 35.4 g
- Carbohydrates 0.8 g
- Sugar 0 g
- Protein 18.2 g
- Cholesterol 109 mg

Herb Pork Chops

Preparation Time: 10 minutes
Cooking Time: 6 hours
Serve: 8

Ingredients:

- 2 lbs pork chops
- 1/4 cup butter, melted
- 1 tbsp fennel seeds
- 1 tbsp dried thyme
- 1 tbsp dried rosemary
- 1 tsp salt

Directions:

1. In a small bowl, mix rosemary, 2 tbsp butter, fennel seeds, thyme, and salt and rub over pork chops.
2. Place pork chops into the slow cooker.
3. Pour remaining oil over pork chops.
4. Cover and cook on low for 6 hours.
5. Serve and enjoy.

Nutritional Value (Amount per Serving):

- Calories 419
- Fat 34.1 g
- Carbohydrates 0.9 g
- Sugar 0 g
- Protein 25.7 g
- Cholesterol 113 mg

Pork Carnitas

Preparation Time: 10 minutes
Cooking Time: 8 hours
Serve: 8

Ingredients:

- 3 lbs pork roast
- 2 tbsp butter, melted
- Pepper
- Salt

Directions:

1. Season pork roast with pepper and salt and place in a slow cooker.
2. Cover and cook on low for 8 hours.
3. Remove meat from slow cooker and shred using the fork.
4. Heat butter in a large pan over medium-high heat.
5. Add shredded meat to the pan and cook for 2-3 minutes.
6. Serve and enjoy.

Nutritional Value (Amount per Serving):

- Calories 378
- Fat 18.9 g
- Carbohydrates 0 g
- Sugar 0 g
- Protein 48.5 g
- Cholesterol 154 mg

Baked Pork Chops

Preparation Time: 10 minutes
Cooking Time: 35 minutes
Serve: 6

Ingredients:

- 6 pork chops, boneless
- 1 tsp dried parsley
- 1/4 cup butter, melted
- Pepper
- Salt

Directions:

1. Preheat the oven to 425 F.
2. Season pork chops with pepper and salt and place on a baking tray.
3. Mix together butter and parsley.
4. Spoon butter mixture over pork chops and bake for 30 minutes.
5. Broil pork chops for 5 minutes.
6. Serve and enjoy.

Nutritional Value (Amount per Serving):

- Calories 324
- Fat 27.6 g
- Carbohydrates 0 g
- Sugar 0 g
- Protein 18.1 g
- Cholesterol 89 mg

Pork Shoulder Roast

Preparation Time: 10 minutes
Cooking Time: 8 hours
Serve: 6

Ingredients:

- 3 lbs pork shoulder roast, boneless and cut into 4 pieces
- 2/3 cup chicken stock
- 1 tbsp fresh oregano
- Pepper
- Salt

Directions:

1. Season meat with pepper and salt and place into the slow cooker.
2. Add oregano and stock over the meat.
3. Cover with lid and cook on low for 8 hours.
4. Remove pork shoulder roast from slow cooker and shred using a fork.
5. Return shredded meat into the slow cooker and stir well.
6. Serve and enjoy.

Nutritional Value (Amount per Serving):

- Calories 585
- Fat 46.3 g
- Carbohydrates 0.6 g
- Sugar 0.1 g
- Protein 38.3 g
- Cholesterol 161 mg

Rosemary Dijon Pork Chops

Preparation Time: 10 minutes
Cooking Time: 10 minutes
Serve: 4

Ingredients:

- 4 pork chops, boneless
- 1/4 cup coconut aminos
- 2 tbsp butter, melted
- 2 tbsp fresh rosemary, chopped
- 1/4 cup Dijon mustard
- 1/2 tsp salt

Directions:

1. In a bowl, mix rosemary, coconut aminos, butter, Dijon mustard, and salt.
2. Add pork chops to the bowl and coat well.
3. Cover and place in the refrigerator for 1 hour.
4. Heat grill over medium-high heat.
5. Place marinated pork chops onto the hot grill and cook for 5 minutes on each side.
6. Serve and enjoy.

Nutritional Value (Amount per Serving):

- Calories 338
- Fat 26.5 g
- Carbohydrates 4.9 g
- Sugar 0.1 g
- Protein 18.8 g
- Cholesterol 84 mg

Pulled Pork Butt

Preparation Time: 10 minutes
Cooking Time: 50 minutes
Serve: 6

Ingredients:

- 3 lbs pork butt, cut into large chunks
- 6 tbsp water
- 1 tbsp oregano
- 1 tbsp butter, melted
- 1 tsp pepper
- 2 tsp salt

Directions:

1. Add the meat into the instant pot and top with butter.
2. In a small bowl, mix oregano, pepper, and salt and sprinkle over meat. Add water and stir well.
3. Secure pot with a lid and select manual and cook for 40 minutes.
4. Once done then allow to release pressure naturally for 10 minutes then release using the quick-release method.
5. Remove meat from pot and shred using a fork.
6. Return shredded meat to the pot and cook on sauté mode for 10 minutes.
7. Serve and enjoy.

Nutritional Value (Amount per Serving):

- Calories 458
- Fat 17.1 g
- Carbohydrates 0.7 g
- Sugar 0 g
- Protein 70.7 g
- Cholesterol 214 mg

Lamb Patties

Preparation Time: 10 minutes
Cooking Time: 10 minutes
Serve: 6

Ingredients:

- 1 lb ground lamb
- 1 lb ground pork
- 2 tbsp butter, melted
- 1 tsp dried rosemary
- 1 tbsp dried oregano
- 1 tbsp dried thyme
- 1 tsp pepper
- 1 1/2 tsp salt

Directions:

1. Add all ingredients into the large bowl and mix until well combined.
2. Make six even shape patties from the meat mixture.
3. Grill patties over medium heat for 5 minutes on each side.
4. Serve and enjoy.

Nutritional Value (Amount per Serving):

- Calories 288
- Fat 12.2 g
- Carbohydrates 1.1 g
- Sugar 0 g
- Protein 41.2 g
- Cholesterol 133 mg

Rosemary Pork Chops

Preparation Time: 10 minutes
Cooking Time: 35 minutes
Serve: 4

Ingredients:

- 4 pork chops, boneless
- 3 garlic cloves, minced
- 1 tsp dried rosemary, crushed
- 1/4 tsp pepper
- 1/4 tsp sea salt

Directions:

1. Preheat the oven to 425 F.
2. Line baking tray with cooking spray and season pork chops with pepper and salt.
3. Mix garlic and rosemary and rub all over pork chops.
4. Place pork chops in a prepared baking tray.
5. Roast pork chops for 10 minutes.
6. Turn oven temperature to 350 F and roast for 25 minutes.
7. Serve and enjoy.

Nutritional Value (Amount per Serving):

- Calories 260
- Fat 20 g
- Carbohydrates 1 g
- Sugar 0 g
- Protein 18.1 g
- Cholesterol 69 mg

Baked Pork Tenderloin

Preparation Time: 10 minutes
Cooking Time: 30 minutes
Serve: 6

Ingredients:

- 2 lbs pork tenderloin

For rub:

- 1/2 tsp oregano
- 1 tbsp garlic powder
- 1/4 tsp pepper
- 1/2 tbsp salt

Directions:

1. Preheat the oven to 425 F.
2. In a small bowl, all rub ingredients and rub over pork tenderloin.
3. Heat oven-safe pan over medium-high heat.
4. Spray pan with cooking spray. Sear pork on all sides until lightly golden brown.
5. Place pan into the oven and roast for about 25-30 minutes.
6. Slices and serve.

Nutritional Value (Amount per Serving):

- Calories 222
- Fat 5.3 g
- Carbohydrates 1.2 g
- Sugar 0.4 g
- Protein 39.8 g
- Cholesterol 110 mg

Chapter 6: Fish & Seafood

Shrimp Stir Fry

Preparation Time: 10 minutes
Cooking Time: 6 minutes
Serve: 4

Ingredients:

- 1 lb shrimp, shelled and deveined
- 3 tbsp butter
- 1/2 tsp dried tarragon
- 1 tsp garlic powder
- 1/2 tsp dried oregano
- 1/4 tsp dried thyme
- 1/4 tsp salt

Directions:

1. Add all ingredients oil to the large mixing bowl and toss until well coated.
2. Melt butter in a pan over medium-high heat.
3. Add shrimp to the pan and cook for 2-3 minutes on each side.
4. Serve and enjoy.

Nutritional Value (Amount per Serving):

- Calories 214
- Fat 10.6 g
- Carbohydrates 2.4 g
- Sugar 0.2 g
- Protein 26.1 g
- Cholesterol 262 mg

Slow Cooked Garlicky Shrimp

Preparation Time: 10 minutes
Cooking Time: 50 minutes
Serve: 8

Ingredients:

- 2 lbs large shrimp, peeled and deveined
- 5 garlic cloves, sliced
- 3/4 cup butter
- 1/4 tsp pepper
- 1 tsp kosher salt

Directions:

1. Add all ingredients except shrimp into the slow cooker and stir well.
2. Cover and cook on high for 30 minutes.
3. Add shrimp and stir well.
4. Cover and cook on high for 20 minutes.
5. Serve and enjoy.

Nutritional Value (Amount per Serving):

- Calories 247
- Fat 17.3 g
- Carbohydrates 2.7 g
- Sugar 0 g
- Protein 21.6 g
- Cholesterol 208 mg

Shrimp Scampi

Preparation Time: 10 minutes
Cooking Time: 13 minutes
Serve: 4

Ingredients:

- 1 lb shrimp, peeled and deveined
- 2 tbsp butter
- 1 fresh lemon, cut into wedges
- 10 garlic cloves, peeled
- 1/4 cup parmesan cheese, grated

Directions:

1. Preheat the oven to 400 F.
2. Add all ingredients except parmesan cheese into the mixing bowl and toss well.
3. Transfer shrimp mixture onto a baking tray.
4. Bake in preheated oven for 13 minutes.
5. Sprinkle with parmesan cheese and serve.

Nutritional Value (Amount per Serving):

- Calories 219
- Fat 9 g
- Carbohydrates 5.8 g
- Sugar 0.4 g
- Protein 28.3 g
- Cholesterol 258 mg

Rosemary Mustard Salmon

Preparation Time: 10 minutes
Cooking Time: 5 minutes
Serve: 4

Ingredients:

- 1 lb salmon
- 3 sprigs rosemary
- 1 cup chicken broth
- 1 tsp mustard powder
- Pepper
- Salt

Directions:

1. Pour broth into the instant pot then place rack in the pot.
2. Place salmon on the rack and sprinkle with mustard powder, rosemary, pepper, and salt.
3. Secure pot with lid and cook on high for 5 minutes.
4. Once done then allow to release pressure naturally then remove the lid.

Nutritional Value (Amount per Serving):

- Calories 165
- Fat 7.6 g
- Carbohydrates 0.5 g
- Sugar 0.2 g
- Protein 23.4 g
- Cholesterol 50 mg

Nutritious Crab Legs

Preparation Time: 10 minutes
Cooking Time: 4 minutes
Serve: 2

Ingredients:

- 1 1/2 lbs crab legs
- 2 tbsp butter, melted
- 1 cup chicken stock
- 3 garlic cloves, minced
- Salt

Directions:

1. Pour the stock into the pot then place the trivet in the pot.
2. Place crab legs on top of trivet and season with salt.
3. Secure pot with lid and cook on high for 4 minutes.
4. Once done then release pressure using the quick-release then remove the lid.
5. Mix together garlic and butter and pour over crab legs.
6. Serve and enjoy.

Nutritional Value (Amount per Serving):

- Calories 455
- Fat 17 g
- Carbohydrates 2 g
- Sugar 0.5 g
- Protein 66 g
- Cholesterol 220 mg

Garlic Mussels

Preparation Time: 10 minutes
Cooking Time: 7 minutes
Serve: 4

Ingredients:

- 1 lb mussels, clean
- 3/4 cup sour cream
- 2 garlic cloves, minced
- 1/2 cup beef broth
- 1/2 tsp dried rosemary
- 1/2 tbsp butter
- Pepper

Directions:

1. Add butter into the instant pot and set the pot on sauté mode.
2. Add rosemary and garlic and cook for a minute.
3. Add pepper and broth and stir well.
4. Add mussels to the steamer basket and place it into the pot.
5. Secure pot with lid and cook on manual low for 1 minute.
6. Once done then release pressure using the quick-release then remove the lid.
7. Transfer mussels to the bowl and top with cream and serve.

Nutritional Value (Amount per Serving):

- Calories 215
- Fat 13 g
- Carbohydrates 7 g
- Sugar 0.7 g
- Protein 15 g
- Cholesterol 51 mg

Ginger Garlic Salmon Fillets

Preparation Time: 10 minutes
Cooking Time: 10 minutes
Serve: 2

Ingredients:

- 2 salmon fillets, skinless and boneless
- For marinade:
- 2 tbsp mirin
- 1 tbsp butter, melted
- 1 tbsp ginger, grated
- 2 garlic cloves, minced

Directions:

1. Preheat the air fryer to 360 F.
2. Add all marinade ingredients into the zip-lock bag and mix well.
3. Add salmon in a zip-lock bag, seal bag, and place it in the refrigerator for 30 minutes.
4. Arrange marinated salmon fillets in the air fryer basket and cook for 10 minutes.
5. Serve and enjoy.

Nutritional Value (Amount per Serving):

- Calories 325
- Fat 16.9 g
- Carbohydrates 9.9 g
- Sugar 4.1 g
- Protein 35 g
- Cholesterol 94 mg

Herb Salmon

Preparation Time: 10 minutes
Cooking Time: 5 minutes
Serve: 2

Ingredients:

- 2 salmon fillets
- 1 tbsp butter, melted
- 1 tsp herb de Provence
- Pepper
- Salt

Directions:

1. Preheat the air fryer to 390 F.
2. Brush salmon fillets with butter and sprinkle with herb de Provence, pepper, and salt.
3. Place salmon fillets in the air fryer basket and cook for 5 minutes.
4. Serve and enjoy.

Nutritional Value (Amount per Serving):

- Calories 293
- Fat 17.1 g
- Carbohydrates 0 g
- Sugar 0 g
- Protein 35.4 g
- Cholesterol 94 mg

Simple Salmon Patties

Preparation Time: 10 minutes
Cooking Time: 7 minutes
Serve: 2

Ingredients:

- 8 oz salmon fillet, minced
- 1 egg, lightly beaten
- 1/4 tsp garlic powder
- Pepper
- Salt

Directions:

1. Preheat the air fryer to 390 F.
2. Add all ingredients into the bowl and mix until well combined.
3. Make patties from mixture and place into the air fryer basket and cook for 7 minutes.
4. Serve and enjoy.

Nutritional Value (Amount per Serving):

- Calories 183
- Fat 9.2 g
- Carbohydrates 0.5 g
- Sugar 0.3 g
- Protein 24.8 g
- Cholesterol 132 mg

Garlic Rosemary Shrimp

Preparation Time: 10 minutes
Cooking Time: 10 minutes
Serve: 4

Ingredients:

- 1 lb shrimp, peeled and deveined
- 1 garlic clove, minced
- 1 tbsp butter, melted
- 1/2 tbsp fresh rosemary, chopped
- Pepper
- Salt

Directions:

1. Preheat the oven to 400 F.
2. Add shrimp and remaining ingredients in a large bowl and mix well.
3. Transfer shrimp mixture into the baking dish and bake for 10 minutes.
4. Serve and enjoy.

Nutritional Value (Amount per Serving):

- Calories 163
- Fat 4.9 g
- Carbohydrates 2.3 g
- Sugar 0 g
- Protein 25.9 g
- Cholesterol 246 mg

Butter Herb Shrimp

Preparation Time: 10 minutes
Cooking Time: 5 minutes
Serve: 4

Ingredients:

- 2 lbs shrimp, peeled and deveined
- 1 tsp dried mixed herbs, chopped
- 1 tbsp garlic, minced
- 1/4 cup butter
- Pepper
- Salt

Directions:

1. Melt butter in a pan over medium heat.
2. Add garlic and sauté for 30 seconds.
3. Add shrimp, pepper, and salt. Cook shrimp for 2 minutes on each side.
4. Add remaining ingredients and stir well and cook for 1 minute.
5. Serve and enjoy.

Nutritional Value (Amount per Serving):

- Calories 375
- Fat 15.4 g
- Carbohydrates 4.3 g
- Sugar 0 g
- Protein 51.9 g
- Cholesterol 508 mg

Seared Scallops

Preparation Time: 10 minutes
Cooking Time: 4 minutes
Serve: 4

Ingredients:

- 1 lb scallops, rinse and pat dry
- 2 tbsp butter, melted
- Pepper
- Salt

Directions:

1. Season scallops with pepper and salt.
2. Heat butter in a pan over medium heat.
3. Add scallops to the pan and sear for 2 minutes then turn scallops to the other side and cook for 2 minutes more.
4. Serve and enjoy.

Nutritional Value (Amount per Serving):

- Calories 180
- Fat 10.1 g
- Carbohydrates 2.7 g
- Sugar 0 g
- Protein 19.1 g
- Cholesterol 53 mg

Baked Shrimp Scampi

Preparation Time: 10 minutes
Cooking Time: 10 minutes
Serve: 4

Ingredients:

- 2 lbs shrimp, peeled
- 3/4 cup butter, melted
- 2 tsp dried oregano
- 1 tbsp garlic, minced
- Pepper
- Salt

Directions:

1. Preheat the oven to 350 F.
2. Add shrimp to a baking dish.
3. In a bowl, whisk together oregano, garlic, butter, pepper, and salt and pour over shrimp.
4. Bake for 10 minutes or until shrimp cooked.
5. Serve and enjoy.

Nutritional Value (Amount per Serving):

- Calories 705
- Fat 53 g
- Carbohydrates 5.3 g
- Sugar 0.7 g
- Protein 52.2 g
- Cholesterol 508 mg

Dijon Salmon Fillets

Preparation Time: 10 minutes
Cooking Time: 20 minutes
Serve: 5

Ingredients:

- 1 1/2 lbs salmon
- 1 tbsp garlic, chopped
- 1 tbsp butter
- 1/4 cup Dijon mustard
- Pepper
- Salt

Directions:

1. Preheat the oven to 375 F.
2. Arrange salmon fillets on a baking tray.
3. In a small bowl, mix together garlic, butter, Dijon mustard, pepper, and salt.
4. Coat salmon top with garlic mixture.
5. Bake for 18-20 minutes.
6. Serve and enjoy.

Nutritional Value (Amount per Serving):

- Calories 215
- Fat 11.8 g
- Carbohydrates 1.5 g
- Sugar 0.2 g
- Protein 27.2 g
- Cholesterol 60 mg

Parmesan Tilapia

Preparation Time: 10 minutes
Cooking Time: 12 minutes
Serve: 4

Ingredients:

- 1 lb tilapia fillets, wash and pat dry
- 1 tbsp butter, melted
- 1 tbsp dried parsley
- 1 cup parmesan cheese, grated
- Pepper
- Salt

Directions:

1. Preheat the oven to 400 F.
2. In a shallow dish, mix parmesan cheese, parsley, pepper, and salt.
3. Brush fish fillets with butter and coat with parmesan cheese mixture.
4. Arrange fish fillets on a baking tray and bake for 10-12 minutes.
5. Serve and enjoy.

Nutritional Value (Amount per Serving):

- Calories 200
- Fat 9.6 g
- Carbohydrates 1.8 g
- Sugar 0.2 g
- Protein 28.6 g
- Cholesterol 71 mg

Baked Tilapia

Preparation Time: 10 minutes
Cooking Time: 20 minutes
Serve: 6

Ingredients:

- 6 tilapia fillets
- 1/2 cup parmesan cheese, grated
- 1/4 tsp dried basil
- 1/4 tsp dried thyme
- 1 tsp garlic, crushed
- 1/2 cup mayonnaise
- Pepper
- Salt

Directions:

1. Preheat the oven to 350 F.
2. Place fish fillets in a baking dish.
3. In a small bowl, mix parmesan cheese, basil, thyme, garlic, mayonnaise, pepper, and salt.
4. Spread cheese mixture on top of fish fillets.
5. Bake for 15-20 minutes.
6. Serve and enjoy.

Nutritional Value (Amount per Serving):

- Calories 194
- Fat 9.2 g
- Carbohydrates 5.2 g
- Sugar 1.3 g
- Protein 23.7 g
- Cholesterol 65 mg

Rosemary Basil Salmon

Preparation Time: 10 minutes
Cooking Time: 15 minutes
Serve: 4

Ingredients:

- 1 lb salmon fillets
- 1 tbsp butter, melted
- 1/4 tsp dried basil
- 3/4 tbsp dried chives
- 1/2 tbsp dried rosemary
- Pepper
- Salt

Directions:

1. Place fish fillets skin side down into the air fryer basket.
2. Mix together butter, basil, chives, and rosemary.
3. Brush fish fillets with butter mixture and air fry for 15 minutes at 400 F.
4. Serve and enjoy.

Nutritional Value (Amount per Serving):

- Calories 180
- Fat 10.6 g
- Carbohydrates 0.3 g
- Sugar 0 g
- Protein 22 g
- Cholesterol 50 mg

White Fish Fillets

Preparation Time: 10 minutes
Cooking Time: 15 minutes
Serve: 2

Ingredients:

- 1 lb white fish fillets
- 1/4 tsp herb de Provence
- 1 tsp garlic, crushed
- 2 tbsp butter, melted
- 2 fresh rosemary sprigs
- 3/4 cup white wine
- Pepper
- Salt

Directions:

1. Preheat the oven to 400 F.
2. Season fish fillets with pepper and salt and place on a baking tray.
3. Pour butter over fish fillets.
4. Place garlic, rosemary, and herb de Provence on top of fish.
5. Roast fish fillets for 10 minutes.
6. Pour wine over fish fillets and continue roast for 5 minutes.
7. Serve and enjoy.

Nutritional Value (Amount per Serving):

- Calories 590
- Fat 31 g
- Carbohydrates 3.7 g
- Sugar 0.7 g
- Protein 56 g
- Cholesterol 175 mg

Crab Cakes

Preparation Time: 10 minutes
Cooking Time: 10 minutes
Serve: 4

Ingredients:

- 8 oz crab meat
- 2 tbsp mayonnaise
- 1 tbsp Dijon mustard
- Pepper
- Salt

Directions:

1. Preheat the air fryer to 370 F.
2. Add all ingredients into the mixing bowl and mix until just combined.
3. Make 4 patties from the mixture and place it into the air fryer basket and cook for 10 minutes.
4. Serve and enjoy.

Nutritional Value (Amount per Serving):

- Calories 165
- Fat 10.7 g
- Carbohydrates 7.1 g
- Sugar 1.6 g
- Protein 10.6 g
- Cholesterol 32 mg

Baked Garlic Halibut

Preparation Time: 10 minutes
Cooking Time: 12 minutes
Serve: 4

Ingredients:

- 1 lb halibut fillets
- 1/4 cup butter, melted
- 1/4 tsp garlic powder
- Pepper
- Salt

Directions:

1. Preheat the oven to 425 F.
2. Place fish fillets in a baking dish.
3. In a small bowl, mix butter, garlic powder, pepper, and salt.
4. Brush fish fillets with butter mixture and bake for 10-12 minutes.
5. Serve and enjoy.

Nutritional Value (Amount per Serving):

- Calories 271
- Fat 15 g
- Carbohydrates 0.3 g
- Sugar 0.1 g
- Protein 30.8 g
- Cholesterol 53 mg

Chapter 7: Snacks

Cheesy Chicken Wings

Preparation Time: 10 minutes
Cooking Time: 2 hours 35 minutes
Serve: 8

Ingredients:

- 2 lbs chicken wings
- 1 1/2 cups parmesan cheese, grated
- 1 tbsp garlic, minced
- 1/2 stick butter, melted
- Pepper
- Salt

Directions:

1. Add chicken wings into the slow cooker.
2. Mix together cheese, garlic, butter, pepper, and salt and pour over chicken wings.
3. Cover and cook on high for 2 hours 30 minutes.
4. Serve and enjoy.

Nutritional Value (Amount per Serving):

- Calories 322
- Fat 17.8 g
- Carbohydrates 1 g
- Sugar 0 g
- Protein 38.4 g
- Cholesterol 128 mg

Grilled Turkey Patties

Preparation Time: 10 minutes
Cooking Time: 10 minutes
Serve: 4

Ingredients:

- 1 lb ground turkey
- 1/2 tsp garlic powder
- 1/2 tsp ginger, powder
- Pepper
- Salt

Directions:

1. Preheat the grill.
2. Add all ingredients into the large bowl and mix well to combine.
3. Make four patties from the mixture and place on hot grill and cook for 5 minutes on each side.
4. Serve and enjoy.

Nutritional Value (Amount per Serving):

- Calories 220
- Fat 8 g
- Carbohydrates 1 g
- Sugar 0.5 g
- Protein 32 g
- Cholesterol 100 mg

Air Fryer Parmesan Chicken Wings

Preparation Time: 10 minutes
Cooking Time: 25 minutes
Serve: 4

Ingredients:

- 1 1/2 lbs chicken wings
- 3/4 tbsp garlic powder
- 1/4 cup parmesan cheese, grated
- Pepper
- Salt

Directions:

1. Preheat the air fryer to 380 F.
2. In a large bowl, mix garlic powder, parmesan cheese, pepper, and salt.
3. Add chicken wings and toss until well coated.
4. Add chicken wings into the air fryer basket and cook for 25 minutes. Shake air fryer basket halfway through.
5. Serve and enjoy.

Nutritional Value (Amount per Serving):

- Calories 385
- Fat 15.3 g
- Carbohydrates 5.6 g
- Sugar 0.4 g
- Protein 53.5 g
- Cholesterol 160 mg

Herb Chicken Wings

Preparation Time: 10 minutes
Cooking Time: 15 minutes
Serve: 4

Ingredients:

- 2 lbs chicken wings
- 1/2 cup parmesan cheese, grated
- 1 tsp Herb de Provence
- Pepper
- Salt

Directions:

1. Add cheese, herb de Provence, pepper, and salt into the large bowl.
2. Add chicken wings into the bowl and toss well to coat.
3. Preheat the air fryer to 350 F.
4. Add chicken wings into the air fryer basket and cook for 15 minutes. Turn chicken wings halfway through.
5. Serve and enjoy.

Nutritional Value (Amount per Serving):

- Calories 475
- Fat 19.6 g
- Carbohydrates 0.8 g
- Sugar 0.1 g
- Protein 70 g
- Cholesterol 211 mg

Chicken Ham Meatballs

Preparation Time: 10 minutes
Cooking Time: 12 minutes
Serve: 4

Ingredients:

- 1/2 lb ground chicken
- 1 egg, lightly beaten
- 1/3 cup onion, diced
- 1/2 lb ham, diced
- 2 garlic cloves, minced
- 1/2 cup swiss cheese, shredded
- Pepper
- Salt

Directions:

1. Add all ingredients into the mixing bowl and mix until well combined. Place in refrigerator for 30 minutes.
2. Preheat the air fryer to 390 F.
3. Remove meatball mixture from refrigerator and make meatballs.
4. Spray meatballs with cooking spray and place in the air fryer basket.
5. Cook meatballs for 12 minutes.
6. Serve and enjoy.

Nutritional Value (Amount per Serving):

- Calories 275
- Fat 13.9 g
- Carbohydrates 4.4 g
- Sugar 0.7 g
- Protein 30 g
- Cholesterol 136 mg

Turkey Meatballs

Preparation Time: 10 minutes
Cooking Time: 10 minutes
Serve: 4

Ingredients:

- 1 egg, lightly beaten
- 1 1/2 lbs ground turkey
- 1/4 tsp dried thyme
- 1/4 tsp dried oregano
- Pepper
- Salt

Directions:

1. Preheat the air fryer to 400 F.
2. Add all ingredients into the mixing bowl and mix until well combined.
3. Make meatballs from the mixture and place it into the air fryer basket.
4. Cook meatballs for 10 minutes. Shake basket halfway through.
5. Serve and enjoy.

Nutritional Value (Amount per Serving):

- Calories 360
- Fat 20 g
- Carbohydrates 2.6 g
- Sugar 1.6 g
- Protein 48.3 g
- Cholesterol 239 mg

Greek Chicken Meatballs

Preparation Time: 10 minutes
Cooking Time: 10 minutes
Serve: 4

Ingredients:

- 1 lb ground chicken
- 1 egg, lightly beaten
- 1 tbsp dried oregano
- 1 1/2 tsp garlic paste
- Pepper
- Salt

Directions:

1. Add all ingredients into the mixing bowl and mix until well combined.
2. Preheat the air fryer to 390 F.
3. Make meatballs from mixture and place into the air fryer basket and cook for 10 minutes.
4. Serve and enjoy.

Nutritional Value (Amount per Serving):

- Calories 240
- Fat 9 g
- Carbohydrates 1.8 g
- Sugar 0.4 g
- Protein 34.5 g
- Cholesterol 142 mg

Turkey Patties

Preparation Time: 10 minutes
Cooking Time: 14 minutes
Serve: 2

Ingredients:

- 8 oz ground turkey breast
- 2 tsp fresh oregano, chopped
- 1 1/2 tbsp butter, melted
- 2 garlic cloves, minced
- 1/4 tsp salt

Directions:

1. Add ground turkey and remaining ingredients into the mixing bowl and mix until well combined.
2. Make 2 patties from the mixture and place it into the air fryer basket.
3. Cook at 360 F for 14 minutes. Turn patties halfway through.
4. Serve and enjoy.

Nutritional Value (Amount per Serving):

- Calories 325
- Fat 19.2 g
- Carbohydrates 4.2 g
- Sugar 1.6 g
- Protein 33 g
- Cholesterol 84 mg

Simple Chicken Wings

Preparation Time: 10 minutes
Cooking Time: 30 minutes
Serve: 2

Ingredients:

- 1 lb chicken wings
- Pepper
- Garlic Salt

Directions:

1. Preheat the air fryer to 400 F.
2. Season chicken wings with pepper and garlic salt and place into the air fryer basket.
3. Cook chicken wings for 30 minutes at 400 F. Flip chicken halfway through.
4. Serve and enjoy.

Nutritional Value (Amount per Serving):

- Calories 435
- Fat 16.8 g
- Carbohydrates 1.1 g
- Sugar 0.3 g
- Protein 66 g
- Cholesterol 202 mg

Cheesy Beef Burger Patties

Preparation Time: 10 minutes
Cooking Time: 15 minutes
Serve: 6

Ingredients:

- 2 lbs ground beef
- 1 cup mozzarella cheese, grated
- 1 tsp garlic powder
- 2 tsp garlic salt

Directions:

1. Preheat the air fryer to 400 F.
2. Add all ingredients into the mixing bowl and mix until well combined.
3. Make patties from meat mixture and place into the air fryer basket and cook for 15 minutes.
4. Serve and enjoy.

Nutritional Value (Amount per Serving):

- Calories 295
- Fat 10.3 g
- Carbohydrates 0.8 g
- Sugar 0.3 g
- Protein 47.3 g
- Cholesterol 138 mg

Herb Lamb Meatballs

Preparation Time: 10 minutes
Cooking Time: 25 minutes
Serve: 4

Ingredients:

- 1 lb ground lamb
- 2 tsp oregano, chopped
- 1 tbsp garlic, minced
- 1 egg, lightly beaten
- 1/4 tsp dried thyme
- Pepper
- Salt

Directions:

1. Preheat the air fryer to 400 F.
2. Add all ingredients into the bowl and mix until well combined.
3. Make small balls from the meat mixture and place it into the air fryer basket and cook for 25 minutes.
4. Serve and enjoy.

Nutritional Value (Amount per Serving):

- Calories 236
- Fat 9 g
- Carbohydrates 1.7 g
- Sugar 0.2 g
- Protein 33.6 g
- Cholesterol 143 mg

Beef Meatballs

Preparation Time: 10 minutes
Cooking Time: 15 minutes
Serve: 4

Ingredients:

- 1 lb ground beef
- 1/4 cup parmesan cheese, grated
- 1 tbsp mozzarella cheese, grated
- 1 tsp garlic powder
- Pepper
- Salt

Directions:

1. Preheat the air fryer to 400 F.
2. Add all ingredients into the bowl and mix until well combined.
3. Make small balls from the meat mixture and place it into the air fryer basket and cook for 15 minutes.
4. Serve and enjoy.

Nutritional Value (Amount per Serving):

- Calories 230
- Fat 8.3 g
- Carbohydrates 1.2 g
- Sugar 0.4 g
- Protein 36.4 g
- Cholesterol 105 mg

Air Fryer Salmon Patties

Preparation Time: 10 minutes
Cooking Time: 7 minutes
Serve: 2

Ingredients:

- 8 oz fresh salmon fillet, minced
- 1/4 tsp dried rosemary
- 1/4 tsp garlic powder
- 1 egg, lightly beaten
- Salt

Directions:

1. Preheat the air fryer to 390 F.
2. Add all ingredients into the bowl and mix until well combined.
3. Make patties from mixture and place into the air fryer basket and cook for 7 minutes.
4. Serve and enjoy.

Nutritional Value (Amount per Serving):

- Calories 185
- Fat 9.2 g
- Carbohydrates 0.4 g
- Sugar 0.3 g
- Protein 24.8 g
- Cholesterol 132 mg

Healthy Salmon Patties

Preparation Time: 10 minutes
Cooking Time: 8 minutes
Serve: 6

Ingredients:

- 14 oz can salmon, drained & flaked with a fork
- 1 egg, lightly beaten
- 1 tsp ginger garlic paste
- Pepper
- Salt

Directions:

1. Preheat the air fryer to 360 F.
2. Add all ingredients into the bowl and mix until well combined.
3. Make patties from mixture and place into the air fryer basket and cook for 8 minutes.
4. Serve and enjoy.

Nutritional Value (Amount per Serving):

- Calories 106
- Fat 4.4 g
- Carbohydrates 0.6 g
- Sugar 0.2 g
- Protein 15.3 g
- Cholesterol 53 mg

Crispy Chicken Wings

Preparation Time: 10 minutes
Cooking Time: 30 minutes
Serve: 2

Ingredients:

- 1 lb chicken wings
- 2 tbsp apple cider vinegar
- 1/4 tsp garlic powder
- 1 tbsp butter, melted
- Pepper
- Salt

Directions:

1. Preheat the air fryer to 360 F.
2. In a bowl, toss chicken wings with garlic powder, butter, pepper, and salt until well coated.
3. Arrange chicken wings in the air fryer basket and cook for 25 minutes.
4. Flip chicken wings and air fry for 5 minutes more.
5. Once done then toss chicken wings with vinegar.
6. Serve and enjoy.

Nutritional Value (Amount per Serving):

- Calories 495
- Fat 24 g
- Carbohydrates 0.6 g
- Sugar 0.3 g
- Protein 65.7 g
- Cholesterol 202 mg

Chapter 8: Salad

Egg Salad

Preparation Time: 10 minutes
Cooking Time: 5 minutes
Serve: 4

Ingredients:

- 12 eggs, hard-boiled
- 1 tbsp Dijon mustard
- 3/4 cup mayonnaise
- Pepper
- Salt

Directions:

1. Separate egg yolks and egg whites.
2. Chop egg whites into small pieces.
3. Add egg yolks, salt, mustard, and mayonnaise in a blender and blend until smooth.
4. Add chopped egg whites in a large bowl then add egg yolk mixture and mix well. Season with pepper and salt.
5. Serve and enjoy.

Nutritional Value (Amount per Serving):

- Calories 363
- Fat 28 g
- Carbohydrates 11.8 g
- Sugar 3.9 g
- Protein 17.2 g
- Cholesterol 503 mg

Shrimp Crab Salad

Preparation Time: 10 minutes
Cooking Time: 5 minutes
Serve: 4

Ingredients:

- 1 lb imitation crab meat, chopped
- 1 tsp garlic powder
- 1 cup mayonnaise
- 1/2 lb shrimp, cooked and chopped
- Pepper
- Salt

Directions:

1. Add all ingredients into the large bowl and mix well.
2. Place salad bowl into the refrigerator for overnight.
3. Serve chilled and enjoy.

Nutritional Value (Amount per Serving):

- Calories 312
- Fat 23 g
- Carbohydrates 1.2 g
- Sugar 0.1 g
- Protein 0.7 g
- Cholesterol 127 mg

Creamy & Tasty Crab Salad

Preparation Time: 10 minutes
Cooking Time: 5 minutes
Serve: 6

Ingredients:

- 3 lbs imitation crab meat, separate pieces of crab
- 1/2 cup mayonnaise
- 1/4 tsp garlic powder
- Pepper
- Salt

Directions:

1. Add all ingredients into the large bowl and stir well.
2. Place salad bowl into the refrigerator for overnight.
3. Serve and enjoy.

Nutritional Value (Amount per Serving):

- Calories 292
- Fat 7.6 g
- Carbohydrates 3.8 g
- Sugar 1.2 g
- Protein 17.5 g
- Cholesterol 50 mg

Delicious Chicken Bacon Salad

Preparation Time: 10 minutes
Cooking Time: 5 minutes
Serve: 2

Ingredients:

- 2 cups chicken breast, cooked and shredded
- 1/2 cup bacon, crumbles
- 1 cup cheddar cheese, shredded
- 1/2 cup sour cream
- 1/4 cup mayonnaise
- Pepper
- Salt

Directions:

1. Add all ingredients into the large bowl and mix well to combine.
2. Serve and enjoy.

Nutritional Value (Amount per Serving):

- Calories 619
- Fat 45.4 g
- Carbohydrates 10.3 g
- Sugar 2.3 g
- Protein 41.7 g
- Cholesterol 169 mg

Chicken Dill Salad

Preparation Time: 10 minutes
Cooking Time: 5 minutes
Serve: 4

Ingredients:

- 1 lb cooked chicken breast, diced
- 1 tbsp fresh dill, chopped
- 2 tsp butter, melted
- 1/4 cup yogurt
- 1/4 tsp pepper
- 1/4 tsp salt

Directions:

1. Add all ingredients into the mixing bowl and toss well to coat.
2. Cover bowl and place in refrigerator until chilled.
3. Serve and enjoy.

Nutritional Value (Amount per Serving):

- Calories 159
- Fat 5 g
- Carbohydrates 1.6 g
- Sugar 1.1 g
- Protein 25.1 g
- Cholesterol 79 mg

Chapter 9: 30-Day Meal Plan

Day 1

Breakfast- Breakfast Waffle

Lunch- Delicious Chicken Soup

Dinner- Baked Pork Chops

Day 2

Breakfast- Bacon Cheese Quiche

Lunch- Shrimp Stir Fry

Dinner- Flavors Beef Skewers

Day 3

Breakfast- Ham Cheese Quiche

Lunch- Cheesy Bacon Chicken

Dinner- Beef Stew Meat

Day 4

Breakfast- Perfect Breakfast Chaffle

Lunch- Slow Cooked Garlicky Shrimp

Dinner- Rosemary Garlic Leg of Lamb

Day 5

Breakfast- Cheese Bacon Chaffle

Lunch- Garlic Chicken

Dinner- Parmesan Lamb Chops

Day 6

Breakfast- Bacon Cheese Mayo Chaffle

Lunch- Shrimp Scampi

Dinner- Dinner Lamb Shoulder

Day 7

Breakfast- Cheddar Cheese Ham Chaffle

Lunch- Herb Chicken Breasts

Dinner- Tasty Flank Steak

Day 8

Breakfast- Bacon Chicken Chaffle

Lunch- Rosemary Mustard Salmon

Dinner- Savory Shredded Beef

Day 9

Breakfast- Cheddar Chicken Chaffle

Lunch- Bacon Herb Chicken

Dinner- Lamb Shanks

Day 10

Breakfast- Tuna Chaffle

Lunch- Nutritious Crab Legs

Dinner- Spiced Pork Tenderloin

Day 11

Breakfast- Mexican Chicken Cheese Chaffle

Lunch- Chicken Casserole

Dinner- Grilled Pork Chops

Day 12

Breakfast- Breakfast Egg Cups

Lunch- Garlic Mussels

Dinner- Steak Bites

Day 13

Breakfast- Sausage Egg Muffins

Lunch- Baked Chicken Wings

Dinner- Tasty Chuck Roast

Day 14

Breakfast- Breakfast Egg Bake

Lunch- Ginger Garlic Salmon Fillets

Dinner- Baked Pork Tenderloin

Day 15

Breakfast- Egg Scrambled

Lunch- Tasty Greek Chicken

Dinner- Garlic Herb Pork Medallions

Day 16

Breakfast- Breakfast Waffle

Lunch- Delicious Chicken Soup

Dinner- Baked Pork Chops

Day 17

Breakfast- Bacon Cheese Quiche

Lunch- Shrimp Stir Fry

Dinner- Flavors Beef Skewers

Day 18

Breakfast- Ham Cheese Quiche

Lunch- Cheesy Bacon Chicken

Dinner- Beef Stew Meat

Day 19

Breakfast- Perfect Breakfast Chaffle

Lunch- Slow Cooked Garlicky Shrimp

Dinner- Rosemary Garlic Leg of Lamb

Day 20

Breakfast- Cheese Bacon Chaffle

Lunch- Garlic Chicken

Dinner- Parmesan Lamb Chops

Day 21

Breakfast- Bacon Cheese Mayo Chaffle

Lunch- Shrimp Scampi

Dinner- Dinner Lamb Shoulder

Day 22

Breakfast- Cheddar Cheese Ham Chaffle

Lunch- Herb Chicken Breasts

Dinner- Tasty Flank Steak

Day 23

Breakfast- Bacon Chicken Chaffle

Lunch- Rosemary Mustard Salmon

Dinner- Savory Shredded Beef

Day 24

Breakfast- Cheddar Chicken Chaffle

Lunch- Bacon Herb Chicken

Dinner- Lamb Shanks

Day 25

Breakfast- Tuna Chaffle

Lunch- Nutritious Crab Legs

Dinner- Spiced Pork Tenderloin

Day 26

Breakfast- Mexican Chicken Cheese Chaffle

Lunch- Chicken Casserole

Dinner- Grilled Pork Chops

Day 27

Breakfast- Breakfast Egg Cups

Lunch- Garlic Mussels

Dinner- Steak Bites

Day 28

Breakfast- Sausage Egg Muffins

Lunch- Baked Chicken Wings

Dinner- Tasty Chuck Roast

Day 29

Breakfast- Breakfast Egg Bake

Lunch- Ginger Garlic Salmon Fillets

Dinner- Baked Pork Tenderloin

Day 30

Breakfast- Egg Scrambled

Lunch- Tasty Greek Chicken

Dinner- Garlic Herb Pork Medallions

Conclusion

This is book is one of the right choices for you if you love to eat meats, steak, ribs, and more. I think many of you are aware of the carnivore diet and its benefits. This book will guide you to adopt a carnivore diet properly. The carnivore diet depends on animal-based products. The diet allows you to consume meats comes from any source. Plant-based foods are strictly avoided in this diet.

The book contains healthy and delicious recipes comes from different categories like breakfast, poultry, beef, pork & lamb, fish & seafood, snack, and salad. All the carnivore diet recipes written in this book are unique and written in an easily understandable form. The recipes written in this book are in standard format with their serving size, exact preparation, and cooking time followed by cooking instructions. All the recipes end with their nutritional value information.

Printed in Great Britain
by Amazon

34053156R00073